I762

STAMFORD HILL TRAMWAYS

including Stoke Newington

Robert J Harley

MP Middleton Press

Cover Picture: The ornamental gardens at Stamford Hill were a feature of Edwardian life in the area. Here car 619 brings up the rear of a trio of tramcars at the terminus south of the crossroads. Passengers have but a short walk to a connecting MET car which would have been stationed on the Middlesex side of the road junction. (J.H.Price Coll.)

Cover Colours: These are similar to the original livery which was applied to the LCC trams.

First published September 1996

ISBN 1 873793 85 5

© *Middleton Press 1996*

Design by - Deborah Goodridge

Published by Middleton Press
Easebourne Lane
Midhurst
West Sussex
GU29 9AZ
Tel: 01730 813169
Fax: 01730 812601

Printed & bound by Biddles Ltd,
Guildford and Kings Lyn

CONTENTS

INTRODUCTION AND ACKNOWLEDGEMENTS

The days of the tramcar in Stamford Hill and Stoke Newington are now long gone - but not forgotten. There are still many who would welcome the return of cheap, reliable public transport which does not cover the streets in diesel fumes. A modern tramway system fits the bill here, but for now we must be content with a delve into the past. This volume completes the coverage of lines north of the Thames which were operated by the London County Council. Readers interested in adjoining areas are directed to companion Middleton Press books: *Walthamstow and Leyton Tramways*, *Aldgate and Stepney Tramways*, *Hampstead and Highgate Tramways* and *Holborn and Finsbury Tramways*.

Again I am very grateful for the assistance of the library of the National Tramway Museum and Rosy Thacker in particular. Reference works consulted include E.R.Oakley's two volume study of the LCC Tramways, C.S.Smeeton's two volumes on the MET, John Barrie's *North London Tramways*, Dr J.Robert's *Les Tramways Parisiens* and various articles from contemporary trade magazines. As always there would be no book without the contributions of many photographers and postcard collectors, past and present. The roll of honour reads thus: F.M.Atkins, A.H.Barkway, W.A.Camwell, C.Carter, A.B.Cross, B.J.Cross, J.B.Gent, J.C.Gillham, D.Jones, D.W.K.Jones, C.F.Klapper, J.H.Meredith, O.J.Morris, H.Nicol, A.D.Packer, R.B.Parr, J.H.Price, H.B.Priestley, R.Rosa, G.N.Southerden, A.J.Watkins, R.J.S.Wiseman.

Car plans have been supplied by Terry Russell and London Transport timetables and notices are by permission of the London Transport Museum, Covent Garden.

GEOGRAPHICAL SETTING

Both Stamford Hill and Stoke Newington lie on the ancient Roman road from London to Cambridge. Until the creation of the Greater London Council in April 1965, Stamford Hill marked the boundary of the former LCC with Middlesex. The area is now totally urban in character, but various parks and the valley of the River Lea break up the housing sprawl emanating from the capital.

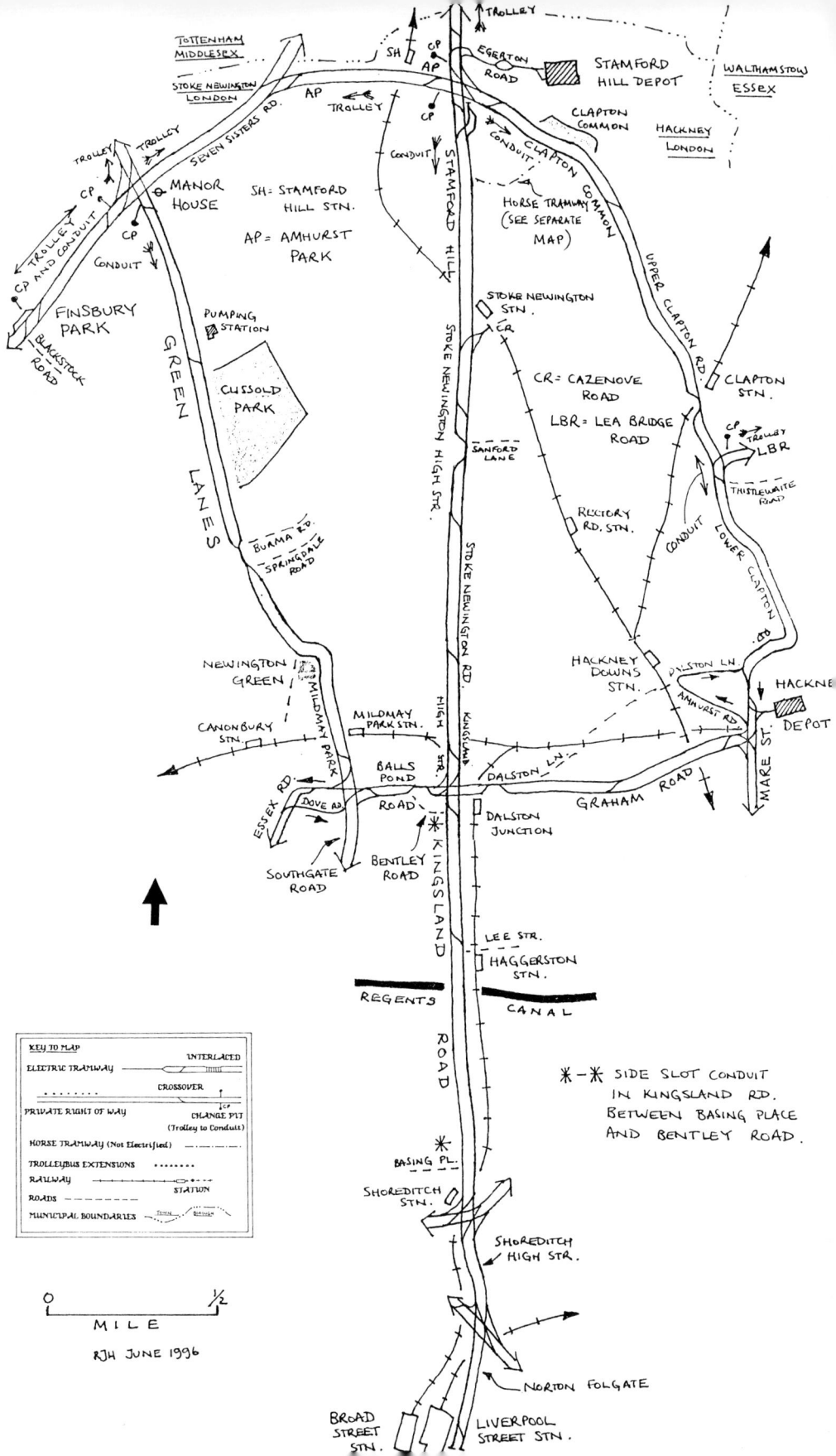

TOTTENHAM
MIDDLESEX

STOKE NEWINGTON
LONDON

TROLLEY

SH
AP

CP
AP

EGERTON
ROAD

STAMFORD
HILL DEPOT

WALTHAMSTOW
ESSEX

SEVEN SISTERS RD.

TROLLEY

TROLLEY

CP

TROLLEY

MANOR
HOUSE

CP

CP

CP AND CONDUIT

CONDUIT

FINSBURY
PARK

BLACKSTOCK
ROAD

SH = STAMFORD
HILL STN.

AP = AMHURST
PARK

CONDUIT

CONDUIT

CLAPTON
COMMON

HACKNEY
LONDON

HORSE TRAMWAY
(SEE SEPARATE
MAP)

STAMFORD HILL

STOKE NEWINGTON
STN.

CR

UPPER CLAPTON RD.

CLAPTON
STN.

CP
TROLLEY

LBR

THISTLEWAITE
ROAD

PUMPING
STATION

CUSSOLD
PARK

GREEN LANES

CR = CAZENOVE
ROAD

LBR = LEA BRIDGE
ROAD

SANFORD
LANE

RECTORY
RD. STN.

CONDUIT

LOWER CLAPTON

BURMA RD.
SPRINGDALE
ROAD

STOKE NEWINGTON HIGH STR.

STOKE NEWINGTON RD.

HACKNEY
DOWNS STN.

DALSTON LN

HACKNEY
DEPOT

NEWINGTON
GREEN

MILDMAY PARK

HIGH STR.

KINGSLAND

AMHURST RD.

MARE ST.

CANONBURY
STN.

MILDMAY
PARK STN.

BALLS
POND
ROAD

DALSTON LN.

GRAHAM ROAD

ESSEX RD.

DOVE RD

BENTLEY
ROAD

DALSTON
JUNCTION

SOUTHGATE
ROAD

KINGSLAND ROAD

LEE STR.

HAGGERSTON
STN.

REGENTS

CANAL

KEY TO MAP

ELECTRIC TRAMWAY — INTERLACED

CROSSOVER

PRIVATE RIGHT OF WAY — CHANGE PIT
(Trolley to Conduit)

HORSE TRAMWAY (Not Electrified)

TROLLEYBUS EXTENSIONS

RAILWAY — STATION

ROADS

MUNICIPAL BOUNDARIES

✳—✳ SIDE SLOT CONDUIT
IN KINGSLAND RD.
BETWEEN BASING PLACE
AND BENTLEY ROAD

BASING PL.

SHOREDITCH
STN.

SHOREDITCH
HIGH STR.

NORTON FOLGATE

BROAD
STREET
STN.

LIVERPOOL
STREET STN.

0 — ½
MILE

RJH JUNE 1996

HISTORICAL BACKGROUND

Horse drawn tramcars operated by the North Metropolitan Tramways Company first appeared in the 1870s on the streets of North London. The Kingsland Road, Stoke Newington line was opened on 17th October 1872; this was followed by the City to Clapton Pond via Hackney service on 23rd July 1873. Mildmay Park and Green Lanes first saw horse trams on 7th May 1874 and Stamford Hill was joined by tramway to Clapton Pond on 3rd April 1875. Kingsland Road to Shoreditch and the City terminus was opened throughout on 5th August 1879. The Green Lanes service was extended to Seven Sisters Road on 4th September 1883. Meanwhile to the north of Stamford Hill construction of the North London Tramways was proceeding apace. These lines, situated mostly in the county of Middlesex, were opened in the following sections: Edmonton to Stamford Hill (horse traction) on 7th June 1881, Stamford Hill to Ponders End (steam traction) on 1st April 1885 and finally the route from Ponders End along Seven Sisters Road to Finsbury Park was inaugurated for steam traction on 12th December 1885. Unfortunately these steam worked lines proved less than satisfactory and the North Metropolitan rescued the ailing company in April 1892, by which time horse cars reigned supreme over the system.

List of services in 1895 - note that vehicles allocated to a particular route were painted in a uniform colour:

Finsbury Park to Moorgate via Upper Street (yellow)
Finsbury Park to Moorgate via Canonbury (brown)
Finsbury Park to Edmonton (blue)
Finsbury Park to Wood Green (yellow)
Stamford Hill to Dock Street (yellow)
Stamford Hill to Holborn (green)
Stamford Hill to Moorgate (red)
Stamford Hill to Edmonton (yellow)
Clapton Swan to Lea Bridge Road (white)
Manor House to Moorgate (green)
Hackney, Well Street to Aldgate (red)
Hackney to Aldersgate (green)
Lea Bridge Road to Bloomsbury (yellow and blue)

The position of the North Metropolitan was also under threat from the newly formed London County Council which set about the compulsory purchase of all horse tramways in its area with a view to electrifying and expanding the system. Lines in Middlesex were acquired by that authority and were converted to electric traction on the overhead wire principle. A new company, the Metropolitan Electric Tramways (MET), operated these lines on behalf of Middlesex County Council. Electric cars started operating on 22nd July 1904 over the sections from Finsbury Park to Wood Green and Manor House to Seven Sisters Corner. The southern extension from Seven Sisters Corner to Stamford Hill was inaugurated on 12th April 1905. The LCC employed the underground conduit method of power supply and Stamford Hill was reached via Stoke Newington and Kingsland Road on 6th February 1907. A section of line in Kingsland Road was experimentally equipped with side conduit. The horse tramway to Finsbury Park which lay in the LCC area was reconstructed as conduit track and was opened on 9th July 1908; there was at first no through running with MET cars. Hackney Road to Mare Street opened on 31st July 1909 and this line was extended on 21st September to terminate at Upper Clapton. Further improvements at Stoke Newington were marked in November 1911 when the Cazenove Road spur came into operation. Other LCC lines followed quickly: Manor House to Balls Pond Road on 3rd August 1912, Balls Pond Road to New North Road on 26th November 1912, Graham Road on 20th March 1913 and Dorset Street on 26th July 1913.

In March 1914 the following local LCC services were in operation:

21 North Finchley to Holborn via Green Lanes and
    Finsbury Park
23 Finsbury Park to Smithfield Market
25 Finsbury Park to Moorgate
27 Seven Sisters Corner to Euston Road (joint with MET)
29 Enfield to Euston Road via Finsbury Park
    (joint with MET)
31 Palmers Green to Euston Road via Finsbury Park
    (joint with MET)
37 Manor House to Aldersgate via Green Lanes
41 Manor House to New North Road via Green Lanes
43 Stamford Hill to Holborn
45 Stamford Hill to Moorgate
47 Stamford Hill to London Docks
49 Stamford Hill to Liverpool Street Station
51 Manor House to Bloomsbury via Green Lanes
53 Clapton Common to Aldgate
55 Leyton to Bloomsbury via Hackney (joint with Leyton)
57 Leyton to Liverpool Street Station via Hackney
    (joint with Leyton)
59 Edmonton to Holborn via Seven Sisters Road
    (joint with MET)
77 Hackney to Dalston Junction
79 Waltham Cross to Smithfield Market via Seven Sisters
    Road (joint with MET)

MET services:
10 Stamford Hill to Edmonton
16 Stamford Hill to Waltham Cross
18 Stamford Hill to Finsbury Park via Bruce Grove and
                                    Wood Green
24 Finsbury Park to Waltham Cross

1952 when diesel buses took over. The local trolleybus routes were abandoned later by London Transport and with the conversion of route 641 (ex-tram 41) on 7th November 1961 the era of electric traction ended.

It will be noted from the above list that through running between LCC and MET cars had resulted in a useful traffic pattern which in some cases still survives in the 1990s LT bus operation. Tracks were connected at Finsbury Park and the first through car from Enfield to Euston Road passed from LCC to MET territory on 1st August 1912. A further change pit from conduit to overhead was constructed by the LCC in April 1915 at Manor House. Through services via Stamford Hill had to wait until the LCC rebuilt Kingsland Road to the more usual centre conduit which MET cars could also negotiate. In the early part of 1920, a change pit was installed at Stamford Hill, but in the event only LCC cars were employed from 2nd June 1920 on an extended service 49 from Liverpool Street Station to Edmonton. The last connecting link in the area was the Amhurst Park overhead wire tramway which opened on 31st March 1924.

The MET guide for 1931 lists the following services:

21 North Finchley to Holborn
27 Edmonton to Euston
29 Enfield to Euston
41 Palmers Green to Moorgate
49 Liverpool Street to Edmonton
51 Muswell Hill to Bloomsbury via Mildmay Park
53 Euston to Aldgate via Finsbury Park
59 Edmonton to Holborn
71 Aldersgate to Aldgate via Finsbury Park, Tottenham,
                          Stamford Hill and Hackney
79 Waltham Cross to Smithfield Market

The formation of London Transport in July 1933 put a question mark over the future of the tramways and it was not long before a policy of trolleybus substitution was settled upon. Soon new traction standards and wires began to encroach on tram routes. The replacement vehicles appeared on route 623 when wiring from Walthamstow to Manor House was opened on 18th October 1936. The conversion in North London was then speeded up and with the disappearance of service 53 on 5th March 1939 all the local trams, bar Kingsway Subway service 33, had departed the scene. The outbreak of the Second World War prolonged the life of service 33, until it too succumbed on 5th April

Ed 4716
L. T. Trams & Trolleybuses
1/-
DAY TICKET
JUL 1941
AUG 1941
SEP 1941
OCT 41
conditions and times of issue see back.

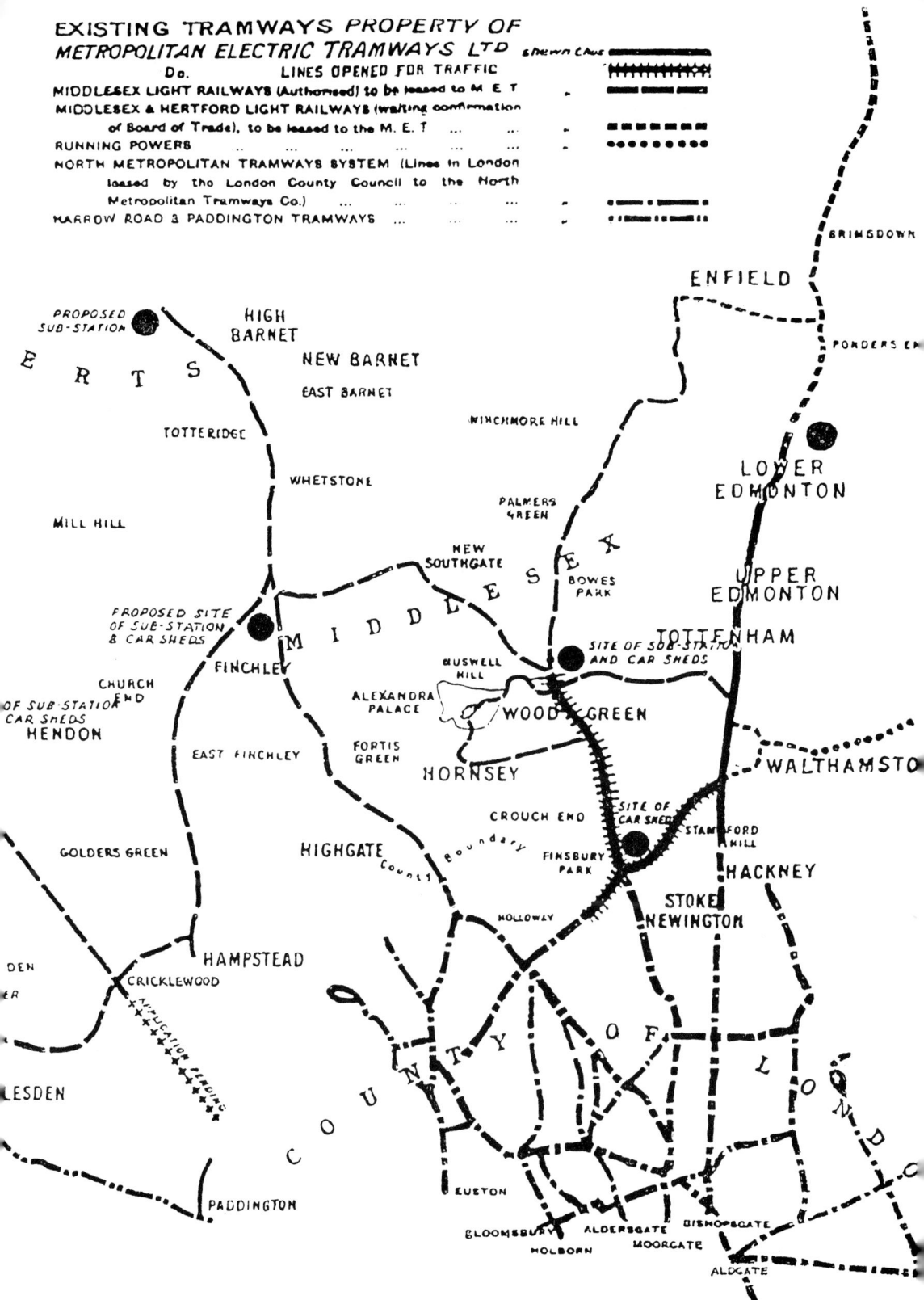

ERTS

PROPOSED SUB-STATION

HIGH BARNET

NEW BARNET

EAST BARNET

ENFIELD

BRIMSDOWN

PONDERS EN

TOTTERIDGE

WHETSTONE

WINCHMORE HILL

LOWER EDMONTON

MILL HILL

PALMERS GREEN

NEW SOUTHGATE

BOWES PARK

UPPER EDMONTON

PROPOSED SITE OF SUB-STATION & CAR SHEDS

MIDDLESEX

MUSWELL HILL

SITE OF SUB-STATION AND CAR SHEDS

TOTTENHAM

FINCHLEY

ALEXANDRA PALACE

WOOD GREEN

CHURCH END

OF SUB-STATION CAR SHEDS

HENDON

EAST FINCHLEY

FORTIS GREEN

HORNSEY

WALTHAMSTO

CROUCH END

SITE OF CAR SHED

GOLDERS GREEN

HIGHGATE

County Boundary

FINSBURY PARK

STAMFORD HILL

HACKNEY

HOLLOWAY

STOKE NEWINGTON

HAMPSTEAD

CRICKLEWOOD

DEN
ER

APPLICATION PENDING

COUNTY

OF

LONDO

LESDEN

PADDINGTON

EUSTON

BLOOMSBURY

HOLBORN

ALDERSGATE

MOORGATE

BISHOPSGATE

ALDGATE

This outline map of tramways in North
London was published in August 1904

STAMFORD HILL

1. This is the initial scene in an enactment of the five ages of tram at Stamford Hill. With suitable apologies to the Bard of Avon, our first entrance on the tramway stage is by North Metropolitan horse car 148 which is working the red route to Moorgate. Although unkind critics from the electric era were wont to point out that the pace of this vehicle was like "snail unwilling", it served its purpose in providing cheap transport for over thirty years. (B.J.Cross Coll.)

2. The next vision of modernity to enhance the streets was this North London Tramways steam tram which is captured on film opposite Ravensdale Road. Truly in 1885 the sighing furnace of this contraption fascinated some folk and frightened others...such as ever was the price of progress.
(North London Tramways)

3. The Metropolitan Electric Tramways reached Stamford Hill in April 1905. Car 279 in this picture dates from around 1911, and these solidly built machines were nicknamed "Dreadnoughts" by the depot staff. (MET)

4. Resplendent in its purple lake and primrose livery, this London County Council electric tramcar arrived on the scene two years after its MET counterpart. Standing in front of car 617 is a bearded inspector for whom all the world's a fare stage and all the men and women merely passengers. (D.Jones Coll.)

5. Our last scene which ends this eventful tramway history features car 1001 in 1938. This tram was reconditioned by LT in October 1935; it was transferred from Thornton Heath to Stamford Hill in September 1937. The smart London Transport red and cream livery belies the fact that in a few months trolleybuses will have taken over and for the tramcar at Stamford Hill it will be mere oblivion - sans rails, sans everything...(W.A.Camwell)

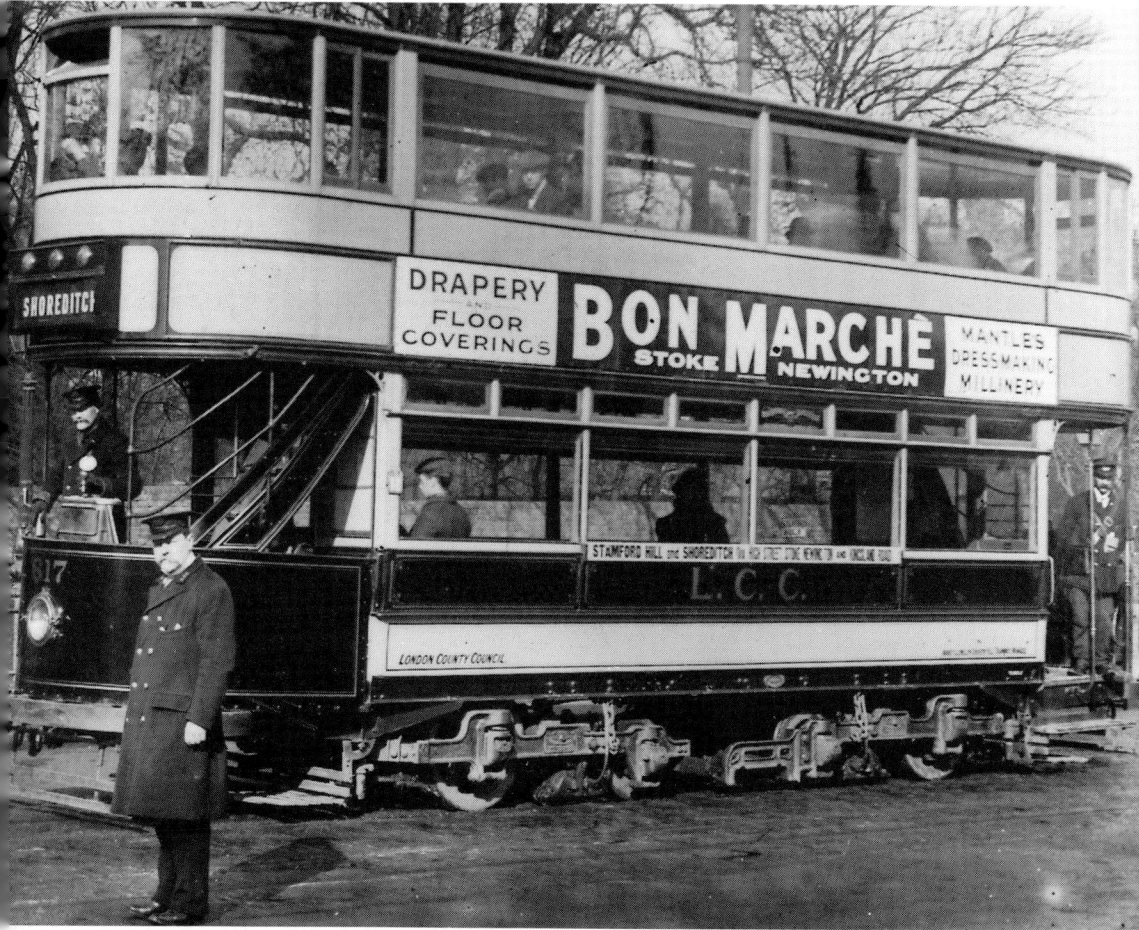

6. After our brief historical resume we now study the layout at street level. Cars on services 43, 47 and 83 are seen on the siding which was opened in 1920. On the main line, a service 53 tram is reversing on a football special to carry spectators to White Hart Lane. Note the taxi on the right of the picture; although this probably offered a more comfortable ride, it could not match the sixpenny (2½p) return tramfare to central London! (D.Jones Coll.)

43
WHITBREAD'S ALE & STOUT
1/- ALL DAY EVERY DAY
OLD STREET
LONDON TRANSPORT

47
83
43
CONSULTING OPTICIAN

7. Out on the main road again with car 1001 and the dank, dismal day probably matches the mood of the local tram enthusiasts as trolley-bus wires seem to be ominously sprouting from all directions. Car 1001 will end its days working from Leyton Depot and will be withdrawn in June 1939. (J.H.Price Coll.)

8. A brighter spectacle of the LCC system in its heyday is now revealed. The leading vehicle in the picture is on service 47 to London Docks, this was "trolleybussed" by LT in February 1939 with the introduction of route 647. Yet another conversion in July 1961 resulted in the 647 being asphyxiated by the diesel fumes of bus 67. (J.H.Price Coll.)

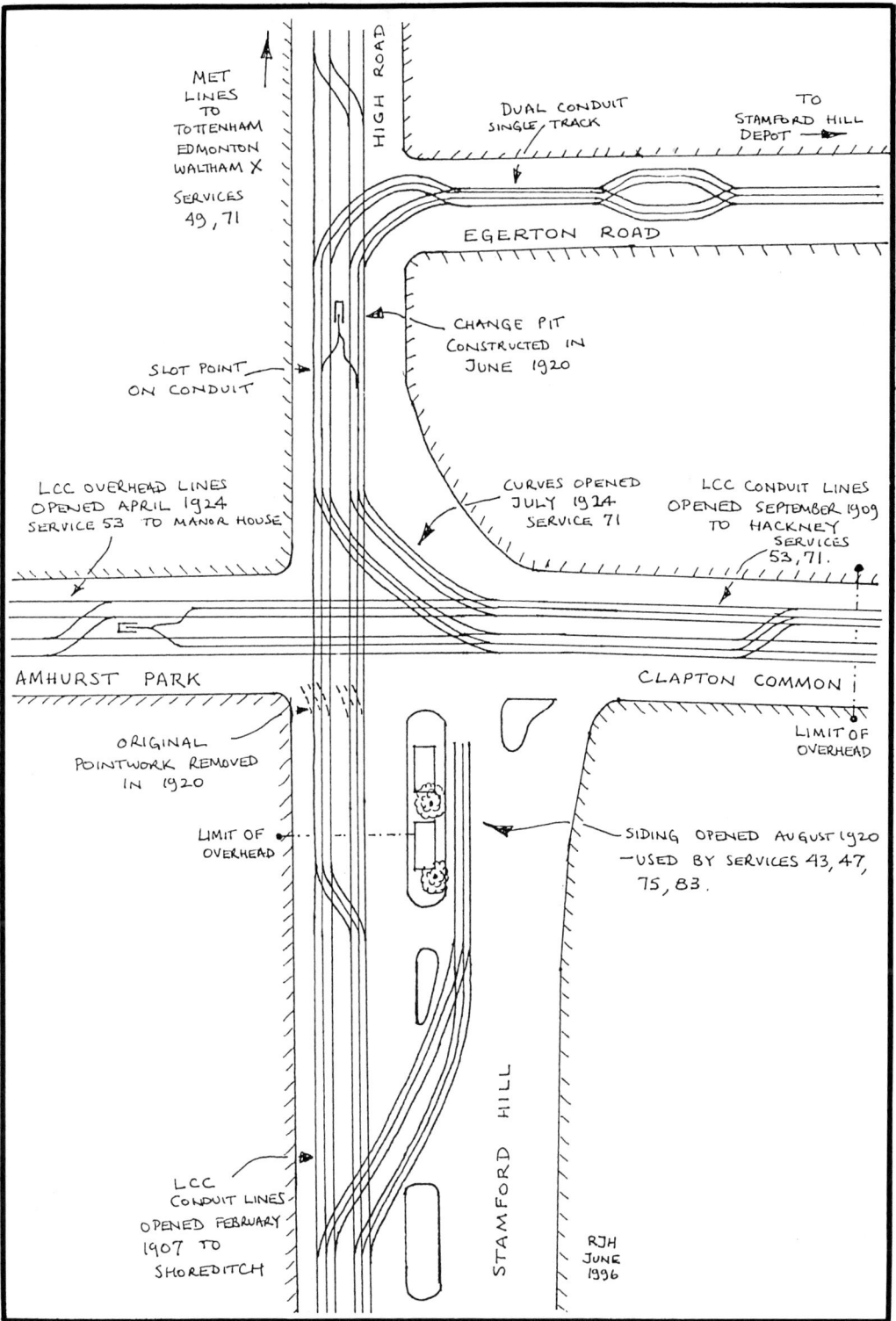

MET
LINES
TO
TOTTENHAM
EDMONTON
WALTHAM X

SERVICES
49, 71

HIGH ROAD

DUAL CONDUIT
SINGLE TRACK

TO
STAMFORD HILL
DEPOT

EGERTON ROAD

CHANGE PIT
CONSTRUCTED IN
JUNE 1920

SLOT POINT
ON CONDUIT

LCC OVERHEAD LINES
OPENED APRIL 1924
SERVICE 53 TO MANOR HOUSE

CURVES OPENED
JULY 1924
SERVICE 71

LCC CONDUIT LINES
OPENED SEPTEMBER 1909
TO HACKNEY
SERVICES
53, 71.

AMHURST PARK

CLAPTON COMMON

LIMIT OF
OVERHEAD

ORIGINAL
POINTWORK REMOVED
IN 1920

LIMIT OF
OVERHEAD

SIDING OPENED AUGUST 1920
-USED BY SERVICES 43, 47,
75, 83.

STAMFORD HILL

LCC
CONDUIT LINES
OPENED FEBRUARY
1907 TO
SHOREDITCH

RJH
JUNE
1996

This diagram shows the final configuration
of tramways at Stamford Hill

9. We move in closer to the terminus and we observe another 53 on football duty. Although the car is empty it will soon fill up on its journey to Tottenham. Spurs in those pre-war days languished in the old second division, but they still attracted crowds of fans who would normally be transported safely by lines of waiting tramcars. (A.D.Packer Coll.)

10. Our vantage point shifts to the pavement outside the shops. Cars 756, 769 and 771 are caught by the camera on 3rd July 1938. In the background a tram on service 71 emerges from Clapton Common. Inspite of their being a frequent tram service, some individuals stubbornly persist in waiting for a bus! (W.A.Camwell)

←

11. Reflections of evening sunshine streaming through the windows of the tram shelter catch our eye as we glance citywards. Car 869 occupies the terminal stub and will shortly return to Shoreditch so that the following tram can move to take its place. Note the services listed on the lintel of the shelter. (C.F.Klapper)

13. Under a spreading London Plane tree we observe that favourite of photographers, car 1001. Note the forest of traction poles and lamp standards which has now invaded this area; at least conduit tramways dispensed with all the paraphernalia associated with the overhead wire stystem. (W.A.Camwell)

←

12. Fashions, both feminine and tramway, feature in this March 1938 view. The plough carrier in the centre of the tram can be clearly seen, as can the trucks and the magnetic brake shoes. These latter enabled the tram to pull up very smartly indeed, much to the chagrin of many a motorist who did not keep a safe distance. Service 83 was replaced by trolleybus 583 on 5th February 1939. (H.Nicol)

14. Pictured at the end of the Stamford Hill siding the motorman of car 1000 makes final checks before departure. Note the stylish traffic lights and the coil of trolleybus traction wire attached to the nearby standard. (J.H.Price Coll.)

Stamford Bazaar, 63 High Road.

Tram Terminus, Stamford Hill.

P.D.W. 68.

15. When the first LCC electric trams turned up in the area, they became objects of local scrutiny. Here a rather stiffly posed policeman is trying hard not to take an interest in newly delivered car 623. The three lights above HOLBORN on the indicator box were illuminated at night in a blank-white-blank sequence for this particular service. From the summer of 1912 service numbers started to appear on the trams and the three light indicators fell into disuse. (J.H.Price Coll.)

16. Points were laid for a proposed spur into Amhurst Park, but the plan remained unfinished and this redundant trackwork was later removed. LCC conduit tracks were extended in 1907 across the junction to the new Stamford Hill Depot; the original MET terminus was then relocated to a crossover just north of Egerton Road. (R.J.Harley Coll.)

17. In this pre-First World War view car 705 is depicted in the midst of assorted LCC staff - motormen and conductors - postmen and the obligatory PC. The advert on the tram's side reminds us that for many of the capital's poorest citizens cocoa remained a staple drink long before "hot chocolate" became fashionable. (A.D.Packer Coll.)

18. Car 613 is loading before it reverses to return to Shoreditch. This vehicle belongs to the E class which is fully described in *Aldgate and Stepney Tramways*. Even though the trams are very popular, bus competition has already reared its ugly head. This was significant at this location side as there was no through running with the adjacent MET trams whose overhead wires can be seen behind car 613. (J.H.Price Coll.)

19. The northern section of service 49 was replaced by trolleybus 649 on 16th October 1938; service 71 was withdrawn on 5th February 1939 without direct trolleybus replacement. Thus we can date this view fairly accurately. Note in the foreground the conduit junction at the intersection with Clapton Common and the tramway overhead which begins at the change pit just in front of the depot connecting track along Egerton Road. (C.F.Klapper)

20. The change pit attendant forks the plough under a southbound car. This scene was repeated many times all over London at locations where trams changed from conduit to overhead. Shortly the motorman will edge his tram forward whilst still drawing power via the trolley pole. He will then halt for the conductor to stow the pole, finally the motorman will switch the car's circuits to take power from the conduit. This service 71 tram will shortly take the left hand track into Clapton Common and on towards Hackney and Aldgate. (J.H.Price Coll.)

71 ALDERSGATE — WOOD GREEN — ALDGATE
Via Goswell Rd., Angel, Upper St., Highbury, Holloway, Finsbury Pk. Manor House, Wood Green, Lordship Lane Bruce Grove, Stamford Hill, Clapton, Hackney, Cambridge Heath, Whitechapel.
Service interval, 6 mins. Journey time, Aldgate—Wood Green 62 mins, Bruce Grove—Aldersgate 50 mins Aldgate — Aldersgate 95 mins.
Sundays, Aldgate—Wood Green only.
Service interval, 6 minutes.

Principal fares, Aldgate—Wood Green 7d.
Wood Green—Aldersgate 6d.

Aldersgate to Aldgate	7	3	7	9	1031	7	3	7	9	11 12	......
Aldersgate to Wood Green	7	3	7	9	1031	7	3	7	9	11 30	......
Aldgate to Aldersgate	5	31	5	54	9 12	5	31	5	54	9 57	......
Aldgate to Wood Green	4	43	5	31	1154	4	43	5	31	12 9	8 42 11
Wood Green to Aldersgate	6	23	6	29	10 6	6	23	6	29	10 50	......
Wood Green to Aldgate	5	15	5	26	1155	5	15	5	26	12 0	8 53 11
Wood Green to Hackney	5	15	5	26	1155	5	15	5	26	12 9	8 53 12
Wood Green to Bruce Grove	4	50	5	15	1155	4	50	5	15	12 9	8 53 12
Hackney to Wood Green	4	14	4	53	1213	4	14	4	53	12 45	8 21 11
Hackney to Aldgate	4	24	5	13	1229	4	24	5	13	12 35	8 24 12
Hackney to Stamford Hill	4	14	4	53	1257	4	14	4	53	1 13	8 21 12
Stamford Hill to Hackney	5	35	5	46	1 19	5	35	5	46	1 29	8 37 1
Stamford Hill to Wood Green	4	28	5	7	1228	4	28	5	7	1 0	8 33 12
Bruce Grove to Wood Green	4	37	5	4	1237	4	37	5	4	1 9	8 42 12
Bruce Grove to Hackney	5	26	5	37	1228	5	26	5	37	12 20	9 3 12

75 STAMFORD HILL — HOLBORN
Via Dalston, Essex Rd., Angel Rosebery Av., Grays Inn Rd.
Service interval, Wkdys only, 68 mins Jny. time, 32 mins.
Through fare 4d.

Stamford Hill to Holborn	5	24	6	0	1048	5	24	6	0 1124 ......
Holborn to Stamford Hill	5	56	6	33	1120	5	56	6	33 1157 ......

All-night service, Stamford Hill-Holborn

21. The trolley pole of car 1274 is already on the wire as the motorman waits at the other Stamford Hill change pit which was situated in Amhurst Park. The date is 23rd July 1938. (H.B.Priestley)

22. From the Upper Clapton direction we observe a 71 on a depot run to Holloway. Interestingly the conductor has been rather effi- cient in putting the trolley up before the tram has reached the change pit on the opposite side of the junction. (C.Carter)

23. MET car 65 stands north of the crossroads. In the background a brace of LCC trams await interchange passengers from the MET car. The open top vehicle leaves potential customers in no doubt as to its destination - WOOD GREEN via WOOD GREEN!! More information is provided in the shape of a blue circle and white cross symbol with a red letter B standing for Bruce Grove. (A.D.Packer Coll.)

24. A somewhat clearer destination is displayed on this splendid tramway convoy. No wonder many Victorians were concerned that steam trams would frighten horses and cause accidents. Contemporary reports suggest that many local children would stand by the roadside and cheer as the Edmonton to Stamford Hill "flyer" hissed and rumbled past. (North London Tramways)

25. The turn from Stamford Hill into Egerton Road is negotiated by this depotbound car. The track here features dual conduit on the single line leading to the car sheds. Behind the tram is Clark's College and a 1930s filling station built to cater for the increasing number of private motorists. (D.W.K.Jones)

26. This E class tramcar has stopped in Egerton Road. Service 75 was withdrawn in February 1939 without direct replacement; the approach track on which the tram is standing was equipped by LT with a single overhead wire as well as the usual conduit. Soon after this July 1938 view was taken, contractors arrived to install four times the amount of overhead for the trolleybuses. (W.A.Camwell)

27. Car 1120 stands sentinel at the gate of Stamford Hill Depot. The building is situated in Rookwood Road and throughout its tramway operational life was used to near capacity. In 1927 the depot complement was recorded at 122 trams. (J.H.Price Coll.)

JK 0194

54B London Passenger 2d Ord
Transport Board (Tramways)

Service 29·41

2	Aldersgate	Enfield	20
3	Percival St., Moorgate or Tottenh'mCtRd	LondonRd (Park Av)	19
		Borden Av or St.	18
4	Angel, Islington, Old St or Morninton Crescent Stn.	Stephens Ch	
		Green	17
C	Essex Rd. Stn. Mintern St. or Camden Town Station	Dean St ·&· Gn.Dragon Ln.	
		Station Rd (Winch- more Hill)	16
6	St. Paul's Rd orBallsP'dRd	Meadow- croft Rd	15
6	Downham Road or Breck nock Rd.	Aldermns Hill or Palmadium	14
7	Albion R I or Nag's Head, Holloway	Myddleton Road	13
		Wood Green Stn	12
8	Lordship Pk or Finsbury Park Station	Turnpike Lane Stn	11
9	Manor House Stn.	Salisbury Hotel, Harringay	10

NOT TRANSFERABLE.

28. The motorman of car 859 waits for this scene to be preserved for posterity before guiding his charge back on to the public highway. (J.H.Price Coll.)

30. The traverser, seen here at the far end of the building, was an important part of most LCC depots. It enabled trams to be moved about and was an efficient means of shunting vehicles on to different tracks. The depot saw its last tramcar in February 1939 and trolleybuses used the facilities until they too were turfed out in 1961, now the place resounds to the roar of diesel exhausts. (W.A.Camwell)

29. The first part of the car sheds was completed in February 1907 and the layout inside eventually consisted of 28 depot tracks some of which held the fleet depicted here. The workforce in each LCC depot was made up of fitters, electricians, brakesmen, traversermen, shunters, truckmen, car washers, coach painters, clerks and storekeepers. During World War I, women were employed to alleviate the labour shortage caused by the flow of men to the colours. It is fair to say that in those days the standard of maintenance and presentation of the vehicles could knock spots off 1990s bus operators! (D.Jones Coll.)

Map of tramways in Stamford Hill
during the horse car era

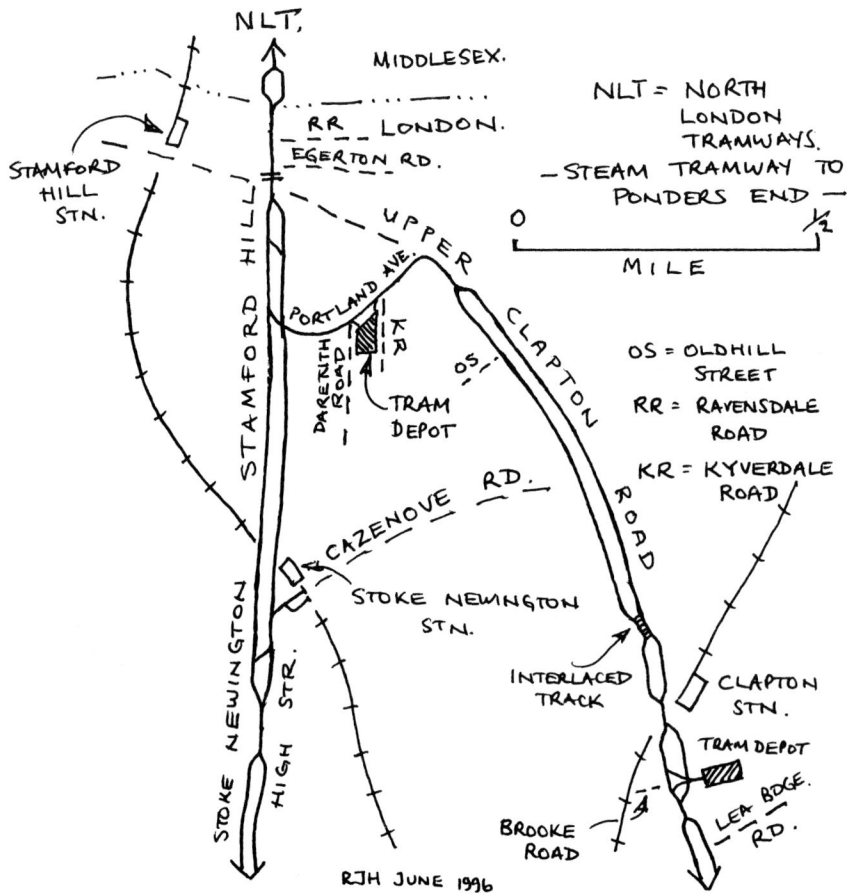

STAMFORD HILL DEPOT.

NLT.

MIDDLESEX.

RR LONDON.
EGERTON RD.

NLT = NORTH
LONDON
TRAMWAYS.
— STEAM TRAMWAY TO
PONDERS END —

STAMFORD
HILL
STN.

UPPER

CLAPTON

PORTLAND AVE.

KR

OS

STAMFORD HILL

DARENTH ROAD

TRAM
DEPOT

0   ½

MILE

OS = OLDHILL
STREET
RR = RAVENSDALE
ROAD
KR = KYVERDALE
ROAD

ROAD

CAZENOVE RD.

STOKE NEWINGTON
STN.

STOKE NEWINGTON

HIGH STR.

INTERLACED
TRACK

CLAPTON
STN.

TRAM DEPOT

LEA BDGE. RD.

BROOKE
ROAD

RJH JUNE 1996

31. The other depot in the Stamford Hill area was the former North Metropolitan horse car sheds in Portland Avenue. The building was later converted into an LCC supplies depot and it is pictured here on 13th June 1959. (J.H.Price)

32. This 43 loads passengers, whilst the driver keeps a watchful eye on yet another cyclist. The lowered windows on the top deck indicate a fine day in prospect. (H.B.Priestley)

33. CARS STOP HERE IF REQUIRED is the message on the stop opposite the tram on service 83 to Moorgate. In London Transport days the through fare on this service was four old pence, the interval between cars four to eight minutes, and the journey time 28 minutes. (J.B.Gent Coll.)

34. We look north from Windus Road on the outskirts of Stoke Newington. Car 612 is still in original condition as it proceeds at a stately pace over rails laid in a granite setted roadway. This surface could be extremely slippery when wet, but on the credit side the setts lasted ages and many of them are still there underneath today's urban highways! (J.B.Gent Coll.)

35. The Weavers Arms stands on the corner of Cazenove Road; on the extreme right of the picture is the single track leading to the Cazenove Road siding. This line leading nowhere had a strange afterlife, because it was reinstated in November 1911 for electric traction as a terminal spur. On the main road it is interesting to note that, were the horse tram and horse bus to return in 1996, they would have no trouble keeping to a timetable, since the average speed of the capital's traffic is now lower than it was in 1905 when this card was posted! (J.B.Gent Coll.)

		MON. to FRI.		SATURDAY		SUNDAY	
		First	Last	First	Last	First	Last
STAMFORD HILL — LONDON DOCKS	Stamford Hill to London Docks	4 50	5 12	11 44	4 50	5 12	11 50	6 10	12 6	......
Via Stoke Newington, Kingsland Rd., Shoreditch, Leman Street Through fare 4d. Service interval 2-4 mins. Journey time, 30 mins.	London Docks to Stamford Hill	5 21	5 44	12 16	5 21	5 44	12 21	6 37	1235	......

		MON. to FRI.		SATURDAY		SUNDAY	
		First	Last	First	Last	First	Last
EDMONTON — DALSTON — LIVERPOOL ST.	Edmonton to Liverpool St. Stn	5 3	5 17	11 23	5 3	5 15	11 26	......
Via Stamford Hill, Kingsland Rd., Shoreditch.	Edmonton to Stamford Hill	5 3	5 17	0	5 3	5 15	0	......
Extended weekday rush hours & Sat. p.m. to Enfield.	Liverpool St. Stn. to Edmonton	5 35	5 47	12* 7	5 35	5 47	12* 5	......
Service interval. Weekdays only, Liverpool St.—Edmonton	Stamford Hill to Liverpool St. Stn	5 11	5 23	11 42	5 11	5 23	11 47	......
3-6 mins., Edmonton—Enfield 6 mins. Journey time	Stamford Hill to Edmonton	4 41	4 53	12*29	4 41	4 53	12*28	......
Liverpool St.—Edmonton 44 mins.,—Enfield 61 mins.	Liverpool St. Stn. to Enfield ......morning	5‡35	5 47	54	5‡35	5 47	42	......
Through fare 6d.	Liverpool St. Stn. to Enfield......afternoon	4 24	4 30	6 30	12 0	12 6	10 30	......
* to Tramway Ave. † Later cars until 1133 to Stamford Hill.	Enfield to Liverpool St. Stn ....morning	6 16	6 22	8 46	6 16	6 22	8 46	......
‡ Earlier car, 5.38 from Stamford Hill.	Enfield to Liverpool St. Stn ....afternoon	4 47	4 53	7 35	1147	1153	11† 9	......

Stoke Newington 1915

MARTABAN ROAD

STRIA PARK

B.M. 85.0

P.O.

Station

Nursery

P.H.

GIBSON GARDENS

S.B.

S.P

Unl.

B.M. 77.3

School

Almshouses

Meth Church

Stamford House

C.R.

SUMMERHOUSE ROAD

Timber Yard

Dispensary

Asylum

OLDHAM PL.

L.B.

Cinema

P.H.

P.H.

GARNHAM STREET

B.M. 83.0

P.H.

Mis. Hall

CLEVEDON STREET

Def.

Hall

School

Met. Boro. Bdy.

SANFORD

P.H.

SMALLEY ROAD

LANE

STOKE NEWIN

Bank

B.M. 87.5

LAWRENCE'S BUILDINGS

Inst.

Bank

P.H.

P.O.

F.E.Sta.

Meth Church Sun.

36. At the northern end of Stoke Newington High Street we catch sight of car 695 which has just passed the Weavers Arms. This tram is working service 45 from Stamford Hill to Moorgate. The 45s had a fitful existence, finally being withdrawn by the LCC on 27th May 1931. (D.Jones Coll.)

37. This early postcard has been "improved" by the publisher to enhance the atmosphere of Stoke Newington High Street. Nevertheless car 622 still presents a majestic spectacle as the only mechanised form of transport in sight. (B.J.Cross Coll.)

38. Shoppers crowd the pavement by Sanford Lane as car 620 halts opposite the Three Crowns on the corner of Church Street. In this Edwardian heyday the chap boarding car 620 would only have needed a penny for the fare to Shoreditch. (B.J.Cross Coll.)

39. Another aspect of the tramway layout which remained constant throughout the horse and electric eras was this stretch of single track in the High Street. The more usual practice on electrification involved street widening to provide double track, but special circumstances prevailed at this location. (B.J.Cross Coll.)

40. A reason for the single track may have been the need to provide parking space for delivery carts and vans. Car 613 is about to clear this section in order to allow a southbound 49 to pass. (D.Jones Coll.)

41. A knot of people stands by the entrance to Farleigh Road as car 707 pulls up at the request stop. Boarding a tramcar usually involved a short walk into the carriageway; this practice became increasingly risky as the volume of motor traffic increased in the 1930s. However this view is from a different age when the term "gridlock" did not belong in the vocabulary of town planners. (D.Jones Coll.)

ROUTE No. 8.

Holborn, Moorgate, Dock Street, and Norton Folgate to Stamford Hill (Electric Traction).

1. Staple Inn.
2. Gray's Inn.
3. Central Markets.
4. St. John's Gate.
5. Clerkenwell Sessions House.
6. Charterhouse.
7. St. Luke's Hospital.
8. Bunhill Fields Burial Ground.
9. Artillery Ground.
10. Wesley's Chapel and Museum.
11. Shoreditch Technical Institute.
12. London Docks.
13. St. Katharine's Docks.
14. Royal Mint.
15. Toynbee Hall.
16. Spitalfields Market.
17. Royal Cambridge Music Hall.
18. Boundary-street Housing Area
19. London Music Hall.
20. Shoreditch Olympia.
21. Shoreditch Town Hall.
22. North Eastern Hospital for Children.
23. Britannia Theatre.
24. Metropolitan Hospital.

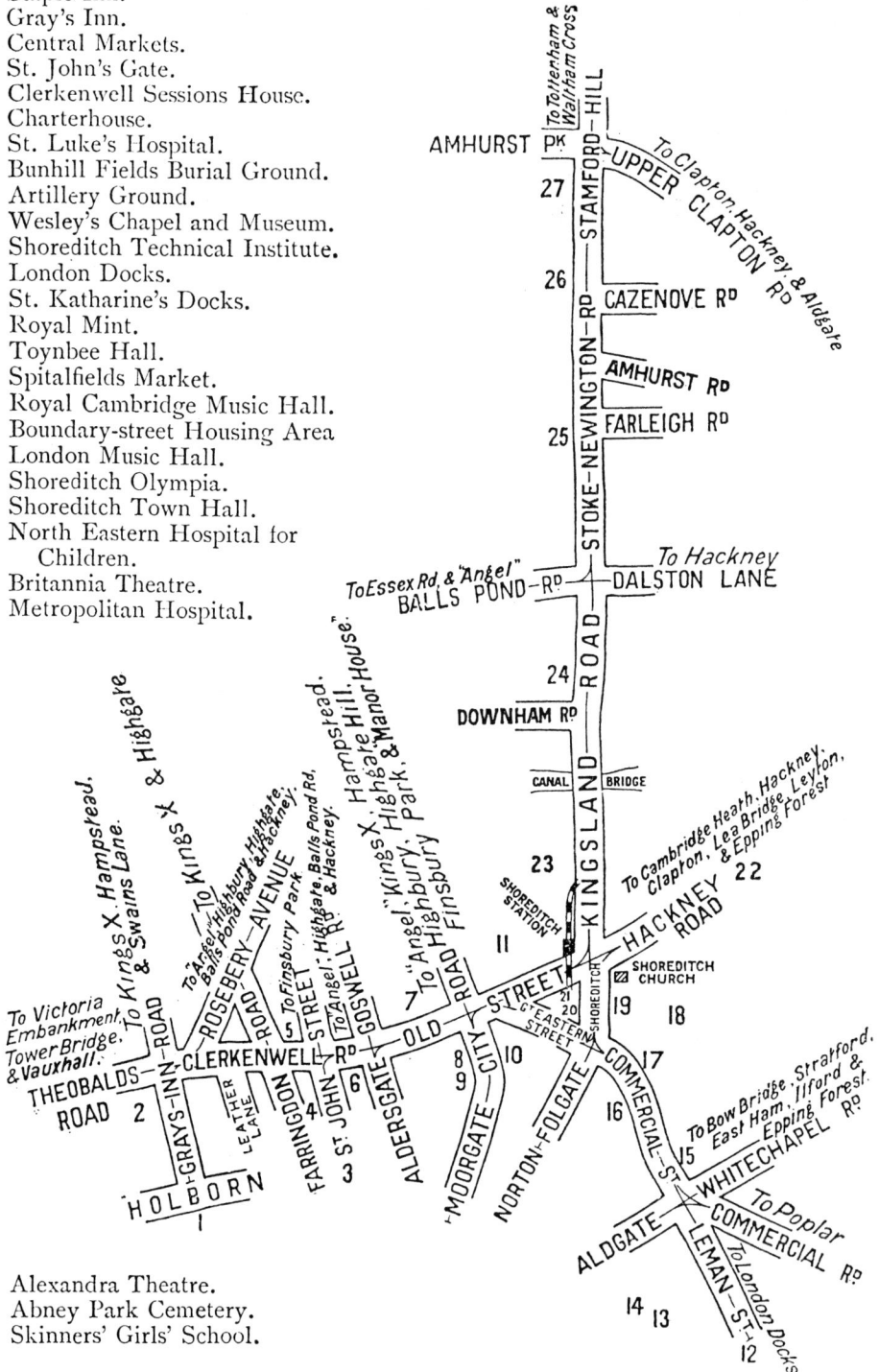

25. Alexandra Theatre.
26. Abney Park Cemetery.
27. Skinners' Girls' School.

Extract from LCC guide 1911

KINGSLAND

42. This postcard was sent on 9th March 1907 and it depicts car 676 as it passes the corner of Bradbury Street.   (R.Rosa Coll.)

Dalston Junction 1915

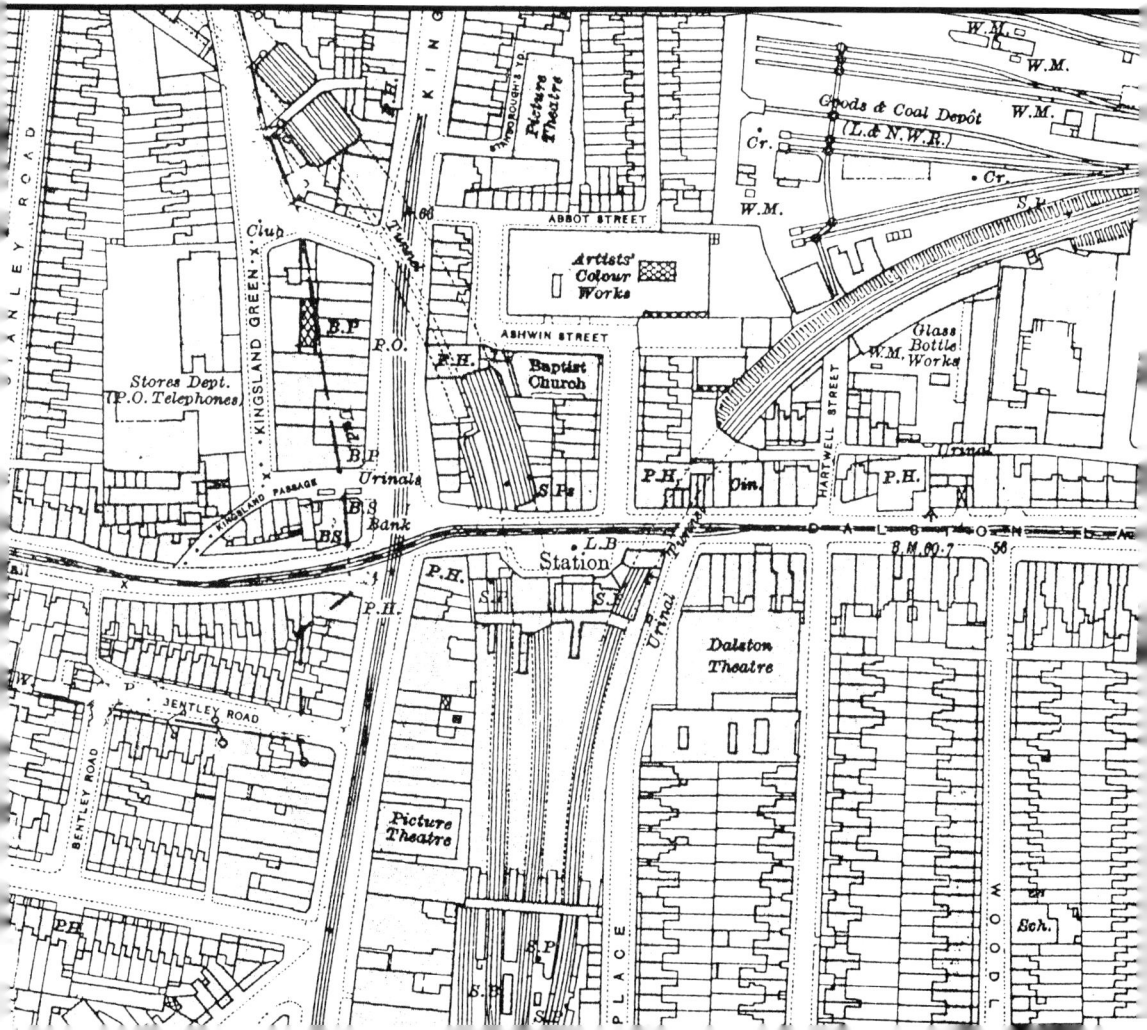

43. Car 609 has just traversed the crossover outside the Kings Arms in Kingsland High Street. Short working cars to Dalston Junction would normally reverse here, but at peak times the crossover at Bentley Road would be called into use. (D.Jones Coll.)

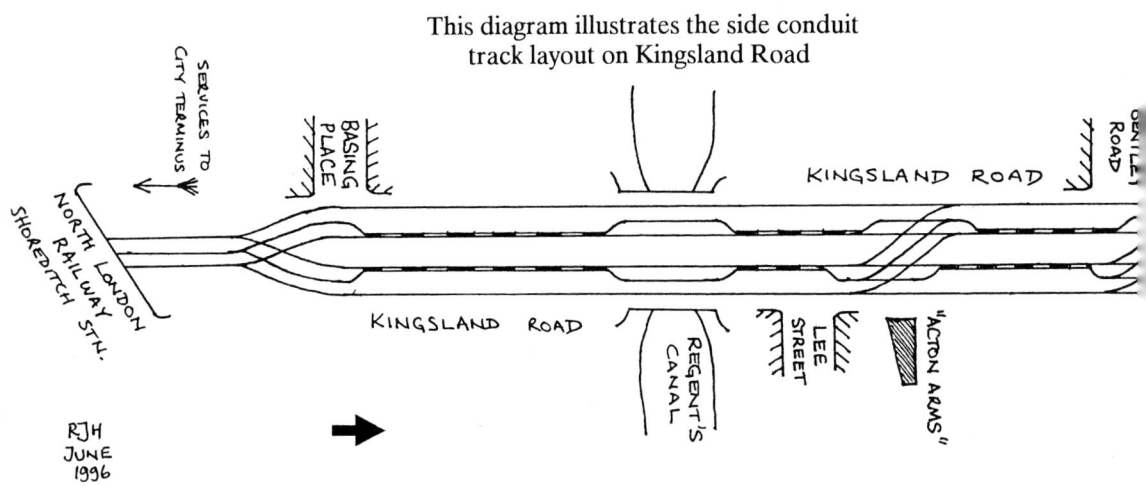

This diagram illustrates the side conduit track layout on Kingsland Road

SERVICES TO CITY TERMINUS

NORTH LONDON RAILWAY SHOREDITCH STN.

BASING PLACE

KINGSLAND ROAD

KINGSLAND ROAD

REGENT'S CANAL

LEE STREET

"ACTON ARMS"

BENTLEY ROAD

KINGSLAND ROAD

RJH
JUNE
1996

Kingsland Road Side Conduit

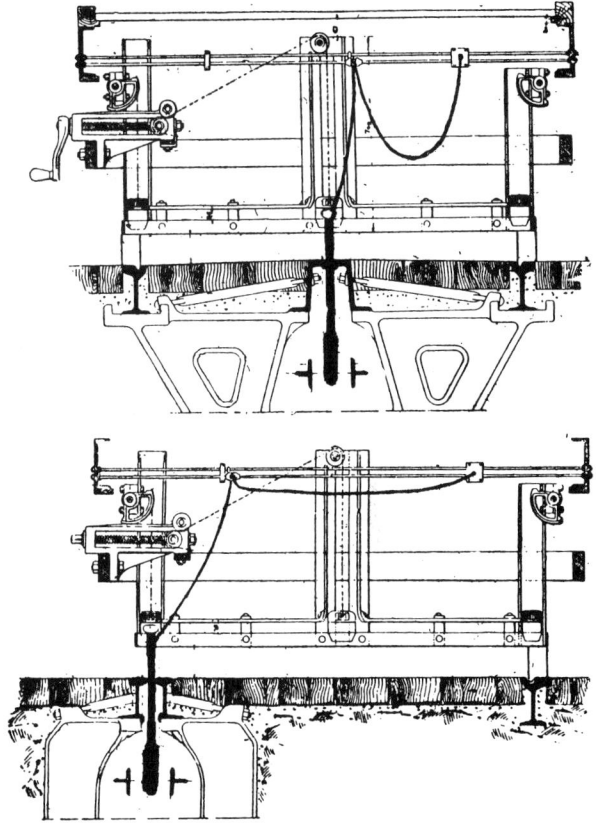

Mention has already been made in the companion volume *Bournemouth and Poole Tramways* of the side conduit which existed in that South Coast resort. This type of conduit was employed experimentally on Kingsland Road. A previous visit to Paris by representatives of the LCC and the Metropolitan Boroughs of Shoreditch and Hackney had resulted in a favourable opinion of the Bastille - Etoile - Pereire route which had opened in 1900. The accompanying picture from *Les Tramways Electriques* by Henri Marechal (published 1902) illustrates the system used at points where the side conduit reverted to a central position. In the background is the Arc de Triomphe. No doubt the elected representatives who sanctioned the Kingsland Road construction were imbued by the spirit of the *Entente Cordiale*, but in practice the side conduit was prone to many problems - wear and tear caused the slot rail to widen and fall out of gauge, street refuse lodged in the conduit and special equipment on the cars was expensive to maintain. The Kingsland Road side conduit was opened on 6th February 1907 and it was replaced by the standard central conduit slot in 1921/2. The last example of this type survived in Paris until route 92 was converted in February 1932. The diagram illustrates the position of the plough in the central and side positions; although this is a Paris car, the London plough apparatus was similar in principle.

44. The side conduit slot was installed in the running rail nearest to the crown of the road. Here at the bridge over the Regent's Canal the slot resumed a central position. (LCC)

→

45. At the corner of Kingsland Road and Mansfield Street the workers take a break for the photographer to record the scene. Manual labour ensured that the yokes which support the side conduit and running rail were positioned precisely. (LCC)

SHOREDITCH TO LIVERPOOL STREET STATION

46. Continuing the theme of trackwork we witness the renewal of the junction at Shoreditch. Car 612 passes under the railway bridge. Shoreditch station was opened in November 1865 and closed in October 1940. Further views of this area are included in *Aldgate and Stepney Tramways*. (H.Nicol)

47. We reach the end of the line for the Stamford Hill routes. Here at Liverpool Street a brand new trolleybus negotiates the terminal loop under the watchful eye of an LT inspector. Tram service 57 disappeared on 11th June 1939. (C.F.Klapper)

Shoreditch 1915

UPPER CLAPTON TO HACKNEY

48. Car 1253 stands at the original Upper Clapton terminus which was situated on the Stamford Hill side of Clapton Common some yards away from the two other tram termini (LCC cars to Stoke Newington and MET cars to Edmonton). Electric trams first reached this spot on 21st September 1909 and the official opening was two days later. In December 1912 the Upper Clapton to Aldgate service received the number 53. (J.H.Price Coll.)

49. Here by Clapton Common we return to the more leisurely days of the horse tram. The North Metropolitan vehicles once took a rather circuitous route via Portland Avenue to reach Stamford Hill. This track and the associated depot were abandoned on conversion to electric traction. (J.H.Price Coll.)

50. On 5th April 1875, horse cars reached the Swan, Upper Clapton, which is seen here behind car 214. The tram is being prepared for the return to Moorgate. Note the advertisements for cocoa (yet again), Hudsons Soap, Promenade Concerts at Covent Garden and Bryant & Mays matches. The match factory with its famous match girls was located not far away at Fairfield Road, Bow. (J.H.Price Coll.)

51. After the connection at Stamford Hill and Amhurst Park was opened in April 1924, it was possible to operate through services from Upper Clapton to Seven Sisters and Wood Green. Here an LCC car on service 71 passes the corner of Oldhill Street. (B.J.Cross Coll.)

52. We return to the same location as in the previous picture, but the time is now around the turn of the century. The tram drawn by two horses seems rather full on the top deck; it is on the Tottenham to Aldgate service. (B.J.Cross Coll.)

3. Car 606 pauses on the single track situated on the bridge over the railway at Clapton Station. One wonders how many passengers alighting here from the LCC trams were looking forward to a good three bob's worth (15p) day trip to sunny Clacton, courtesy of the Great Eastern Railway. (D.Jones Coll.)

4. We enter Lower Clapton Road in company with car 603. It is about to pass the crossover opposite Thistlewaite Road. Note the local picture house is showing "The Spitfire of Seville" starring Hedda Nova! (J.B.Gent Coll.)

55. Car 635 approaches the crossover seen in the previous photo. This is not far from Clapton Pond, the original July 1873 horse tramway terminus. (D.Jones Coll.)

56. The electric trams in Hackney pioneered a one way system round the town centre. Here we look along the single track in Amhurst Road. Car 1217 was photographed sometime around 1910. More pictures of the Hackney tramways are contained in companion volume *Aldgate and Stepney Tramways*. (J.B.Gent Coll.)

57. We make our way back to Mare Street where we note a horse car on the Lea Bridge Road service. Other tram services in Lea Bridge Road are described in *Walthamstow and Leyton Tramways*. To the right of the tram just by the Pianoforte Manufacturer is Bohemia Place and the connection to Hackney Depot. (J.B.Gent Coll.)

58. The ancient tower of the parish church still dominates the scene as cars 1199 and 1198 pass in the shadow of the North London Railway bridge. Just in front of the lad pushing the crate of beer bottles is the connecting curve to the horse tramway in Graham Road. This was opened for electric traction on 20th March 1913. (J.B.Gent Coll.)

59. This is an 1880s view of Hackney railway bridge. In the foreground two horse cars with "knifeboard" seating on the top deck are about to wend their way south. From 1883 onwards the North Metropolitan embarked on a car rebuilding programme which included the introduction of transverse "garden" seats in place of the original "knifeboard" back-to-back variety. (B.J.Cross Coll.)

		MON. to FRI.		SATURDAY		SUNDA	
		First	Last	First	Last	First	La
55 **LEYTON — HACKNEY — BLOOMSBURY** Via Bakers Arms, Clapton, Hackney, Cambridge Heath, Shoreditch, Old Street, Clerkenwell Road. Service interval, Weekdays only, Bloomsbury—Leyton (Bakers Arms) 4–8 mins. Leyton (Bakers Arms)—Leyton Stn. (L.N.E.R.) 5–8 mins. Leyton Station—Wanstead Flats 5 mins. Journey time, Bloomsbury—Leyton (Bakers Arms) 48 mins.,—Leyton Stn. 58 mins.,—Wanstead Flats 64 mins. Through fare 5d. Extended to Wanstead Flats Saturday afternoons and evenings.	Leyton Stn. (L.N.E.R.) to Hackney Stn.....	6 31	6 39	1123	6 32	6 42	1159	
	Leyton Stn. (L.N.E.R.) to Bloomsbury	6 31	6 39	11 8	6 32	6 42	1119	
	Bloomsbury to Wanstead Flats				1254	1 4	1042	
	Bloomsbury to Leyton Stn.(L.N.E.R.)........	5 53	6 7	1031	6 6	6 15	1042	
	Bloomsbury to Leyton (Bakers Arms)........	4 5	4 51	1119	4 5	4 51	1123	
	Bloomsbury to Hackney Station............	4 5	4 51	1223	4 5	4 51	1226	
	Bloomsbury to Clapton (K'hall Road).......	4 5	4 51	12 0	4 5	4 51	12 7	
	Hackney Stn. to Bloomsbury	3 26	4 20	1153	3 26	4 20	12 0	
	Hackney Stn. to Leyton (Bakers Arms)	3 47	4 31	1146	3 48	4 31	1151	
	Leyton (Baker Arms) to Bloomsbury........	4 5	4 55	1125	4 5	4 55	1144	
	Leyton (Bakers Arms) to Hackney Stn	4 5	4 55	12 3	4 5	4 55	1210	
	Clapton (K'hall Rd.) to Bloomsbury........	3 20	4 14	1147	3 20	4 14	1154	
	Hackney Station to Wanstead Flats........				1 27	1 47	1110	
	Wanstead Flats to Hackney Station.........				2 9	2 19	1148	
	Wanstead Flats to Bloomsbury				2 9	2 19	11 9	

57 **CHINGFORD MOUNT — LIVERPOOL ST. STN.** Via Walthamstow, Hoe St., Leyton, Clapton, Hackney, Cambridge Heath, Shoreditch. Service interval 4–8 mins. Journey time, 55 mins. Through fare 6½d.	Chingford Mount to Liverpool St Station....	6 37	6 42	1122	6 36	6 41	1124	7 35	11 2
	Chingford Mount to Leyton (Bakers Arms)....	6 37	6 42	1229	6 36	6 41	11 16	7 35	12 2
	Liverpool St. Stn. to Chingford Mount......	5 40	6 0	1138	5 40	6 0	1148	7 40	11 4
	Liverpool St. Stn. to Leyton (Bakers Arms)..	5 40	6 0	1213	5 40	6 0	1216	7 40	12 1
	Leyton (Bakers Arms) to Chingford Mount..	6 16	6 28	1210	6 14	6 34	1224	7 17	12 1
	Leyton (Bakers Arms) to Liverpool St. Stn.	5 3	5 23	1140	5 4	5 24	1142	7 6	11 4

60. This tram is working along the Dalston Lane/Graham Road section in 1895. Car 419 is a green liveried vehicle on the Hackney to Aldersgate service; the through fare was tuppence! (B.J.Cross Coll.)

WALTHAM X — KINGS X. — HOLBORN
Via Ponders End, Edmonton, Bruce Grove, Manor Hse., Finsbury Pk., Holloway. Service Interval 6-8 mins.
Journey time, 75 mins.
Through fare 1/-.
Sundays, Edmonton Town Hall—Holborn only

	MON. to FRI.		SATURDAY		SUNDAY	
	First	Last	First	Last	First	Last
Edmonton to Holborn	4*25	4*47 11 42	4*25	4*47 11 38	8*43	11 22 ......
Holborn to Edmonton	5 20	5 38 1 3	5 20	5 38 1 3	9 30	1 3 ......
Waltham Cross to Holborn	6 35	6 41 11 20	6 35	6 41 11 15	......	......
Holborn to Waltham Cross	5 20	5 38 10 12	5 20	5 38 10 19	......	......
* From Tramway Avenue 6 mins earlier.						
† To Tramway Avenue.						

61. The steam service from Edmonton to Finsbury Park opened on 12th December 1885, but after a couple of years the pounding given to the track by the locomotives began to result in derailments and interrupted services. The final straw came in 1890 when the tramway company went into liquidation. The last steam tram ran on 31st July 1891 and the safe, reliable horse trams from the North Metropolitan took over. (North London Tramways)

63. Late in the tramway era LT car 2170 climbs the hill near Amhurst Park corner. Trolleybus wires are already in position and route 659 will replace trams on 16th October 1938. (C.Carter)

62. All the marvel and wonder of the new electric era is apparent in this photograph of MET car 31 on the Finsbury Park service. The local press was full of glowing reports extolling the virtues of cheap, reliable and mechanically sound transport - in contrast to the ill fated steam cars. Electric propulsion presented a "clean" image, a fact which is just as valid today. (J.B.Gent Coll.) ←——————

64. After the formation of London Transport in July 1933 certain Walthamstow eight wheel cars, similar to car 2044 depicted here, were transferred for duties on North London services which needed speeding up. The extra power of the ex-Walthamstow "rockets" more than matched the new MET Feltham type trams. The tram shown in this view has just arrived at Manor House. (J.H.Price Coll.)

68. The next arrival after the two LCC cars is MET car 275 which has positioned itself by the staircase leading to Manor House Station booking hall. Unfortunately this ultra modern tramway layout also became a casualty of London Transport anti-tram mania and the whole lot was abandoned in 1939. The loading islands were subsequently demolished in 1951. (G.N.Southerden)

69. LCC car 1154 is photographed from the westbound platform. This vehicle looks distinctly old fashioned when compared to the up to date tram/tube interchange facility. For far too long some parts of the London tramway system were dogged by lack of investment and official reluctance to modernise cars with the addition of a driver's windscreen. (LCC)

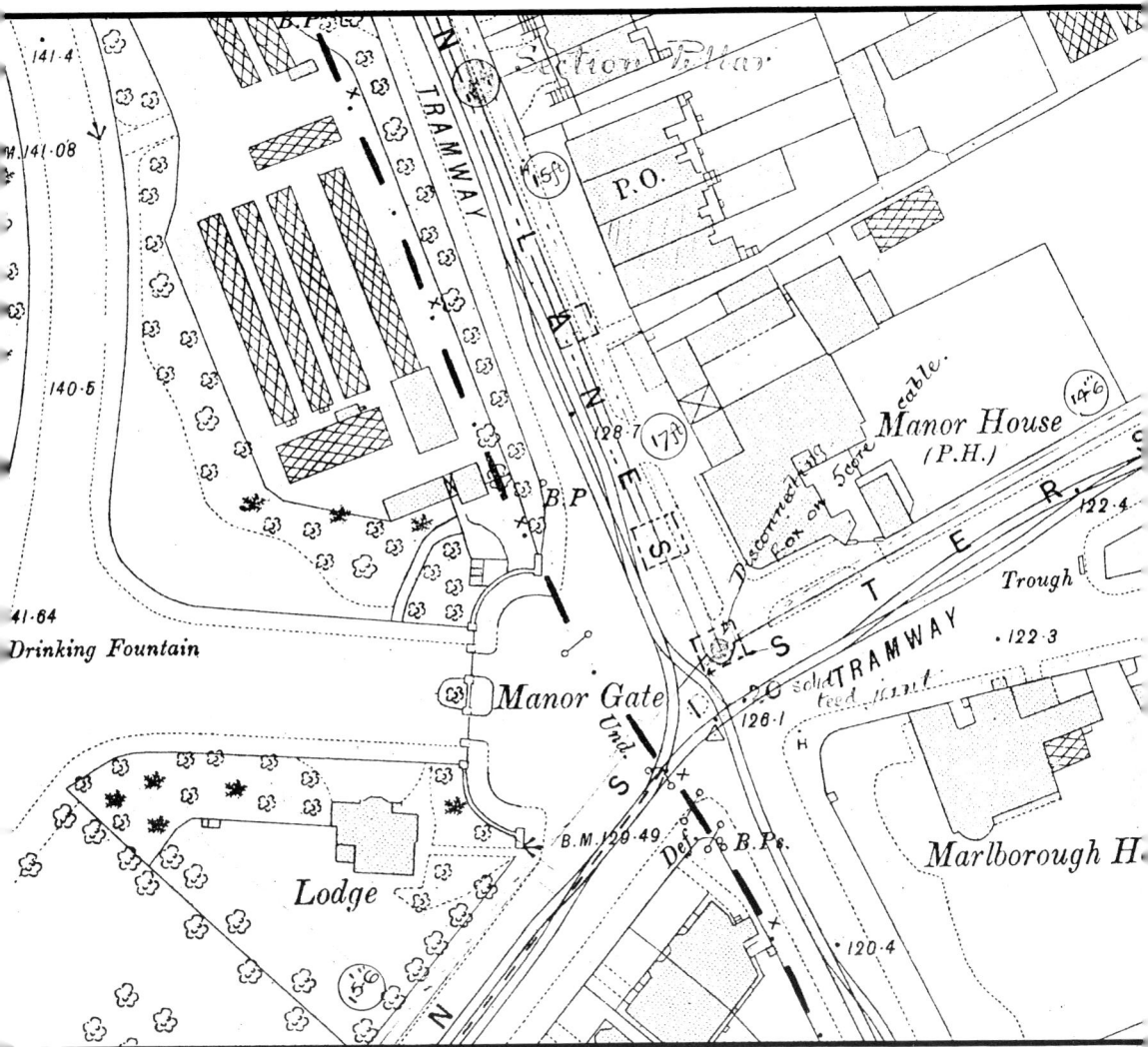

Manor House 1894. This map extract is from the original drawings used by MET Construction Engineers - hence the references to underground feeder cables for the new electric tramways.

70. It is 2.45pm one afternoon in 1929 and D type car 191, rebuilt in 1921 from a three window lower deck, passes C1 type car 201. This latter car is working service 29T to Enfield Town. This suffix letter was used to distinguish MET tram routes, but the custom later fell into disuse. (F.Merton Atkins)

72. Cars 2196 (ex-MET car 264) and 1269 pause awhile as the crews exchange pleasantries. The ex-LCC vehicle on service 41 is working off route, on a depot run to Holloway. (G.N.Southerden)

71. The conduit/overhead change pit on the western side of Manor House road junction is viewed from the top deck of an approaching tram. This change pit was opened on 30th April 1915. The lights turn green and a motorist accelerates away to turn right in front of a London bound tram which has just left the loading island. (H.Nicol)

FINSBURY PARK

73. One of the disadvantages of tramway travel, at least in the horse era, was the enforced wait for an approaching car to clear a single track section. Here, on Seven Sisters Road in Finsbury Park, the tram on the right can now proceed towards London as its opposite number has now regained the double track. (R.J.Harley Coll.)

74. All aboard for Wood Green as the two equine powered rivals line up for the off along Seven Sisters Road. The tracks from Finsbury Park to Wood Green and Seven Sisters Corner were opened for electric traction on 22nd July 1904. (J.B.Gent Coll.)

75. Passengers have to change between two forms of traction at the Middlesex/London county boundary by Blackstock Road. On the left of the picture is the horse tram depot. The horse tram is on the Finsbury Park to Euston Road service. MET car 6 is working to Wood Green whilst a sister vehicle is rostered on the Edmonton service. (R.J.Harley Coll.)

76. LCC conduit tracks arrived in Finsbury Park in the summer of 1908. Four years later a temporary conduit/overhead change pit was installed opposite Blackstock Road and through services 31 (Euston Road to Palmers Green), and 29 (Euston Road to Enfield) were introduced over connecting rails to the MET. The section from Finsbury Park to Manor House was later reconstructed for both conduit and trolley. We observe in this scene a line of four MET vehicles with an LCC car on service 21 heading the group. (R.J.Harley Coll.)

MANOR HOUSE
GREEN LANES

77. An LT official is observed cleaning out a point blade at a crossover just south of the Manor House Junction. Two enthusiast specials are about to set off on a farewell tour of the Kingsway Subway lines which closed on 5th April 1952. More information on this tour is contained in *Holborn and Finsbury Tramways*. (R.J.S.Wiseman)

⟶

78. Service 33 was the last tramway connection to Manor House. Here car 1988 ekes out its last days before replacement by the 171 bus. (J.H.Meredith)

79. We now look southwards along Green Lanes. In the foreground car 2198 is caught on camera just as the motorman is guiding his charge forward to the change pit. The conversion of service 41 to trolleybuses took place on 8th May 1938. (A.B.Cross)

80. The fairytale towers of the water pumping station loom above car 1272. This self proclaimed architectural folly dates from 1854-6 and was designed by Chadwell Mylne. The mixture of styles, a combination of French chateau and Gothic castle, helps set the tone for this section of Green Lanes. On the left of the picture a clover leaf LCC stop sign completes the scene. (R.J.Harley Coll.)

81. Car 194 is seen by Clissold Park on 26th June 1951. Note the familiar 1950s shape of the Daimler LCC ambulance which just conceivably may be ringing its bell - no wailing sirens in those days - to pass the Whitbread delivery dray and the 33 tramcar. (R.J.S.Wiseman)

82. Something or someone on the tram has attracted the cyclist's attention as he passes one of the entrances to Clissold Park. The gloomy weather matches the occasion, as this is 5th April 1952, the last day of service 33. (R.J.S.Wiseman)

CLISSOLD WARD

Green Lanes 1915

83. Some of the properties in Green Lanes had seen better days when this view was taken in the late 1920s. Car 1135 rumbles past a proto- type of today's "wheelie" rubbish bin. (J.B.Gent Coll.)

84. On the far right of the picture a policeman shelters under the canopy of Allardyce's Post and Telegraph Office on the corner of Spring- dale Road. In the distance a tram enters the single track section by Burma Road. Note the wonderful array of small shops. (B.J.Cross Coll.)

NEWINGTON GREEN

85. Our journey now takes us to Newington Green at the corner of Albion Road; this area was once bisected by the boundary between the two former Metropolitan Boroughs of Stoke Newington and Islington. The horse tramway from Balls Pond Road to Newington Green opened on 7th May 1874. It was closed for reconstruction on 11th November 1911, and the new electric cars started on 3rd August 1912. (B.J.Cross Coll.)

86. Newington Green is a pleasant spot once associated with Daniel Defoe of Robinson Crusoe fame. Double track will enable this Manor House bound horse car to pass its opposite number on the service to Moorgate. The quality of life round here was certainly enhanced by the carefully tended trees and open spaces. (B.J.Cross Coll.)

87. Some half a century on from the previous view and the tramway era has but a few hours to run. Car 1939 will later make the pilgrimage to New Cross Depot and will meet a fiery end at Penhall Road scrapyard before the year of 1952 is out. What a waste! (R.J.S.Wiseman)

MILDMAY PARK TO BALLS POND ROAD

88. Mildmay Park seen around 1900 is almost devoid of traffic save for the distant horse tram by Newington Green. In these circumstances it would seem that a single tramtrack is adequate to maintain the service. (J.H.Price Coll.)

89. This picture presents an interesting contrast with the previous view. There are now two forms of electric traction on show; in just over nine years from the date of this shot even the trolleybus will have departed, victim of the 141 diesel bus. Note that the houses have given up their ornamental railings in the wartime scrap metal drive. (R.B.Parr/NTM)

Mildmay Park 1915

90. Car 1998 is on the one way section in Balls Pond Road which was used only by westbound trams. Shortly the car will swing on to the double track at the start of Essex Road. More scenes of this location are to be found in *Holborn and Finsbury Tramways*. (R.J.S.Wiseman)

ROUTE No. 9. Bloomsbury and Aldgate to Stamford Hill (Clapton Common) (Electric Traction).

1. Gray's Inn.
2. Clerkenwell Sessions House.
3. St. John's Gate.
4. Smithfield Market.
5. The Charterhouse.
6. St. Luke's Hospital.
7. Bunhill Fields.
8. Honourable Artillery Company.
9. Wesley's Chapel.
10. Shoreditch Technical Institute.
11. Shoreditch Town Hall.
12. Shoreditch Olympia.
13. Boundary-street Housing Area.
14. North-Eastern Hospital for Children.
15. Toynbee Hall.
16. Whitechapel Art Gallery.
17. Stepney Borough Museum.
18. Pavilion Theatre.
19. London Hospital.
20. Foresters' Music Hall.
21. Bethnal Green Gardens.
22. Bethnal Green Museum.
23. Lady Holles' School.
24. Hackney Empire.
25. Hackney Old Church.
26. Hackney Institute.
27. Hackney Downs Secondary School.

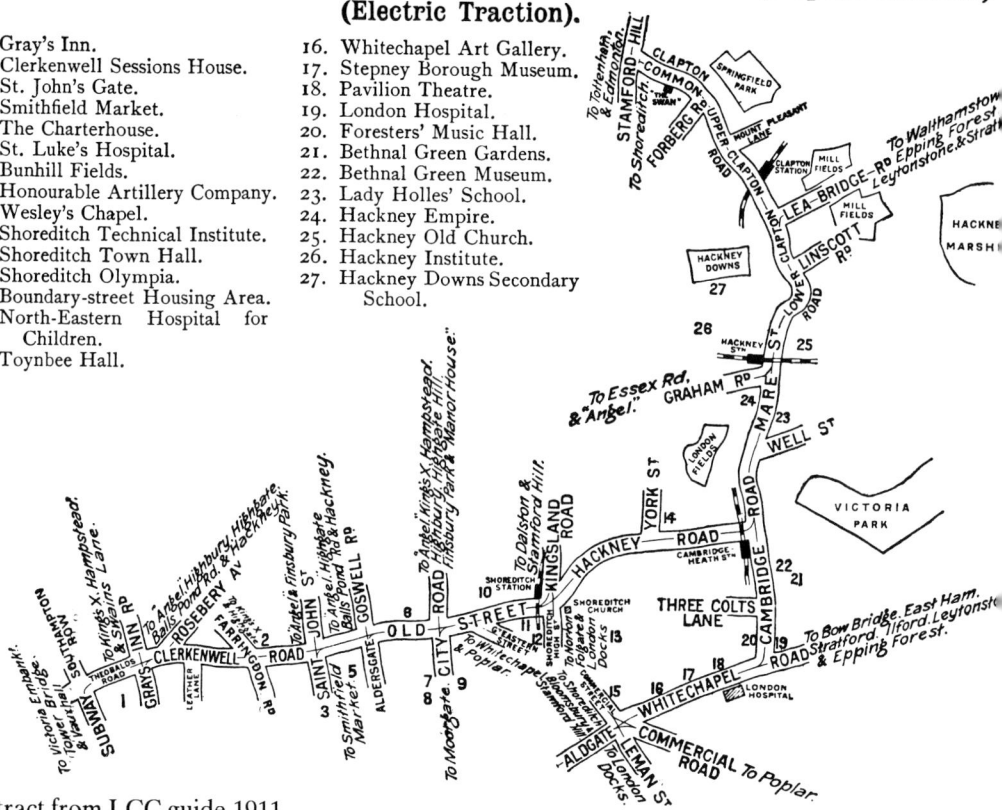

Extract from LCC guide 1911

ROUTE 33	West Norwood - Westminster - Islington - Manor House	P.M. times are in heavy figures

Via Norwood Road, Dulwich Road, Brixton Water Lane (return via Morval Road and Dalberg Road), Brixton Road, Kennington Park Road, Kennington Road, Westminster Bridge, Kingsway Subway, Theobalds Road, Rosebery Avenue, Upper Street, Essex Road, Dove Road, (return via Balls Pond Road), Mildmay Park, Green Lanes.

RAILWAY STATIONS SERVED : West Norwood, Tulse Hill, Herne Hill, Brixton, Oval, Lambeth North, Westminster, Charing Cross, Holborn, Angel, Canonbury, Mildmay Park, Manor House.

Service interval : WEEKDAYS, 6-8 minutes (evening 12 minutes) ; SUNDAY, 12 minutes (evening 15 minutes)

		WEEKDAYS				SUNDAY		
	*	First		Last		First		Last
WEST NORWOOD *Thurlow Arms*	4 51	5 11		9 2	9 37	8 26		9 2	9 40
Herne Hill *Dulwich Road*	4 59	5 19		9 10	9 45	8 33		9 10	9 48
Kennington Gate	5 15	5 35		9 26	10 1	T10 15	8 47		9 26	10 4
Waterloo Bridge *Embankment*	5 29	5 49		9 41	10 16	10 19	8 59		9 41	10 19
Bloomsbury *Southampton Row*	5 32	5 52		9 44	10 19	10 22	9 2		9 44	10 22
Islington *Angel*	5 43	6 3		9 55	10 30	10 33	9 10		9 55	10 33
St. Pauls Road *Canonbury*	5 50	6 10		10 2			9 17		10 2	
MANOR HOUSE *Station*	6 2	6 22		10 14			9 28		10 14	
MANOR HOUSE *Station*		5 12		9 57	10 20		8 23		9 57	10 20
St. Pauls Road *Canonbury*		5 23		10 8	10 31		8 34		10 8	10 31
Islington *Angel*		5 30		10 16	10 39		8 41		10 16	10 39
Bloomsbury *Southampton Row*		5 41		10 26			8 49		10 26	
Waterloo Bridge *Embankment*		5 44		10 29			8 52		10 29	
Kennington Gate		5 58		10 44			9 4		10 44	
Herne Hill *Dulwich Road*		6 14		11 0			9 18		11 0	
WEST NORWOOD *Thurlow Arms*		6 22		11 8			9 25		11 8	

EARLY MORNING JOURNEYS

Norwood *Depot* to Savoy Street, SUNDAY at 6 33 a.m.
Bloomsbury to Highgate, SUNDAY at 5 0 a.m.
Bloomsbury to Manor House, WEEKDAYS at 4 40, 5 24 a.m. ; SUNDAY at 6 3, 7 5, 8 6 a.m.
Islington *Angel* to Manor House, WEEKDAYS at 3 51, 4 34, 5 0, 5 14, 5 40 a.m. ; SUNDAY at 8 2, 8 8, 8 32, 8 44, 8 56 a.m.
Islington *Sub Station* to Manor House, WEEKDAYS at 5 25 a.m.
Manor House to Bloomsbury, WEEKDAYS at 4 12, 4 55 a.m. ; SUNDAY at 6 34, 7 38 a.m.
Highgate to Bloomsbury, SUNDAY at 5 32 a.m.
Holloway *Depot* to Bloomsbury, SUNDAY at 4 31 a.m.
Holloway *Depot* to Islington *Sub Station*, WEEKDAYS at 5 8 a.m.
Holloway *Depot* to Islington *Angel*, WEEKDAYS at 3 32, 4 15, 4 41, 4 55 a.m. ; SUNDAY at 7 43, 7 49, 8 13, 8 25, 8 37 a.m.
Waterloo Bridge to Norwood *Depot*, SUNDAY at 7 13 a.m.

LATE NIGHT JOURNEY

Islington *Angel* to Holloway *Depot*, DAILY at 10 29, 10 41 p.m.

T—Time at Scotland Yard.   *—Special early journey.

91. Our last view on our tramway journey sees car 1996 in Dove Road, formerly Dorset Street. This was one way for eastbound trams. The chalked inscriptions on the dash tell their own story - most ordinary Londoners loved their trams and would miss the cheap fares and the reassuring presence of a very environmentally friendly form of transport.
(R.J.S.Wiseman)

ROLLING STOCK

Tramway enthusiasts in the Stamford Hill and Finsbury Park areas were particularly fortunate in the variety of tramcars on display. The former LCC classes have been described in other Middleton Press volumes. In this book we tackle MET types B,G,H - note that the LCC referred to their vehicles by *class* whereas the MET employed the word *type*.

Type B cars 1-35, Type B1 cars 36-70, Type B2 cars 3-5, 7, 9-11, 13, 15, 16, 19, 24, 26, 27, 30, 34.

Built in 1904 by Brush of Loughborough, the original type B cars were to a double deck, open top design. They ran on Brush BB maximum traction trucks. Bench seating in the lower saloon was for 30 passengers and transverse seating on the top deck accommodated 38. Cars 36-70 (designated B1) differed in having part transverse seating for 24 in the lower

deck. In the early days of the system they were stationed at Wood Green and Edmonton depots, although some members of this type later migrated to Finchley, Hendon and Stonebridge Park depots. Sixteen type B trams were reconstructed at Hendon in 1912-16 as top covered cars and they were reclassified type B2. Various other improvements involved higher powered motors and new electrical equipment. Cars 2, 12, 22, 31 and 46 were taken out of service in 1926 to become works cars. The rest of the open top cars were gradually withdrawn from 1931 onwards and the last four were broken up by London Transport in 1935. The covered top cars of type B2 were often to be found on services 60 and 62 operating out of Finchley and Stonebridge Park depots. They were acquired by LT in 1933 and went for scrap in 1935/6.

92. This April 1927 view shows car 51 in almost original condition except for the addition of extended top deck guard rails to protect passengers from a flailing trolley pole. The livery of the dashes and waist panels is bright, signal red and the rocker panels and windows are painted in ivory. The title METROPOLITAN ELECTRIC TRAMWAYS LTD is in black letters. On the waist panel is the Middlesex coat of arms. (G.N.Southerden)

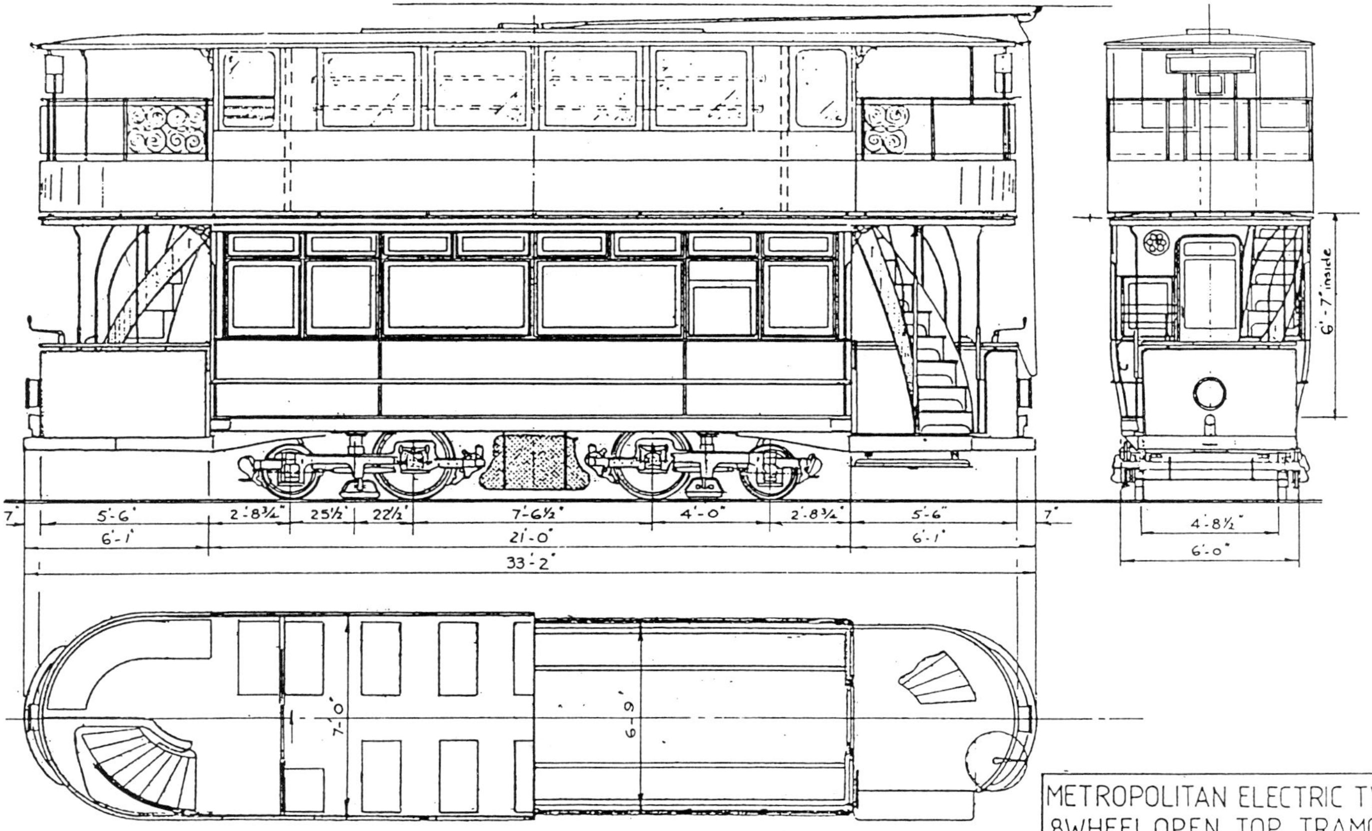

METROPOLITAN ELECTRIC TWYS.
8WHEEL OPEN TOP TRAMCAR

TYPE: 'B2'   SCALE: 4 mm = 1 Foot

DRAWING No. TC 148

BODY: Brush El Eng Co Ltd. Seating 30 (longitudinal) 44 on + 38. 60

TRUCKS - Brush Max Ton. Wheels 21¾'. 34½' dia. Wh. Axles Journals

EQUIPMENT 2 GE Motors - 58 Contactors BTH-B16. Trolley - BTH

6'·7' inside

4·8½'
6·0'

7'
5·6'
6·1'
2·8¾'
4·0'
7·6½'
21·0'
33·2'
2·8¾'
25½' 22½'
5·6'
6·1'
7'

6·9'

7·0'

93. B/2 car 19 is seen in July 1927. Note the intricate wrought iron work surrounding the open balconies and the unequal window layout of the top deck which does not match up with the window arrangement of the lower saloon. The car to the rear is a MET type A tram which now looks distinctly archaic in design. (G.N.Southerden)

94. A definite retrograde step was the replacement of the wrought iron grills with sheet metal screens. This supposed "upgrade" took place around 1931 and the resulting appearance of car 11 makes the vehicle look distinctly top heavy. METROPOLITAN now appears in gold letters shaded black on the waist panel; the county arms has been moved to the rocker panel. (G.N.Southerden)

Type G

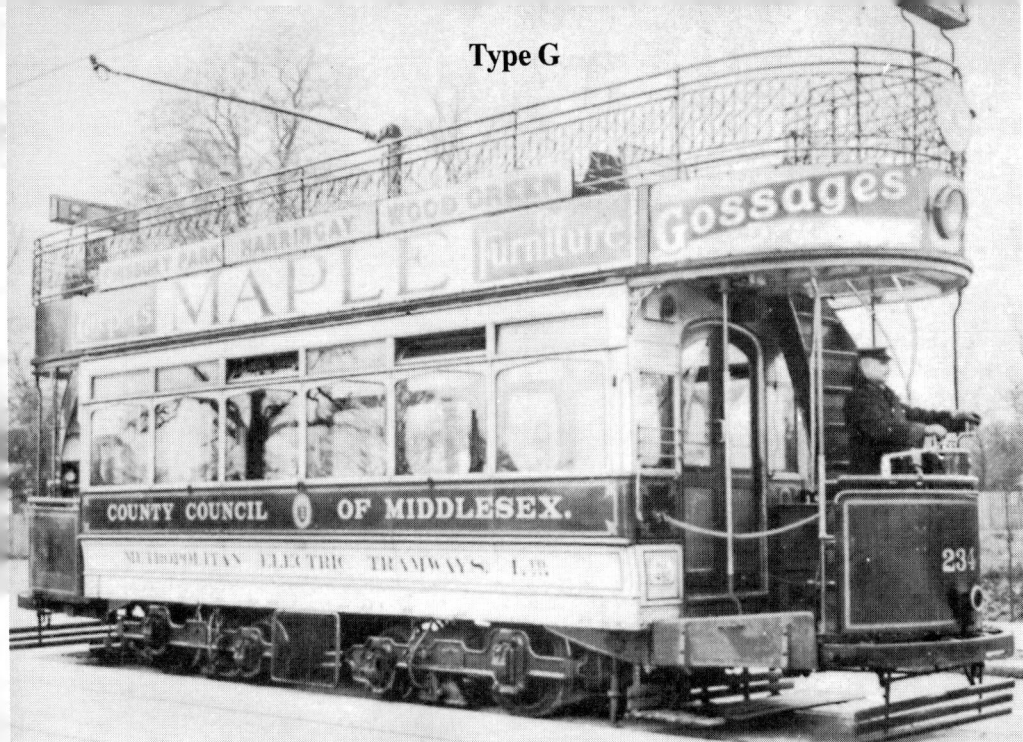

95. Car 234 is shown in original state with COUNTY COUNCIL OF MIDDLESEX in gold letters on the waist panel. (MET)

96. The type G trams were quite stylish and this impression was enhanced by the smart livery and the fine, clean condition in which they were sent out on the road. MET car 233 was later renumbered LT car 2278 and it was sent for scrap in November 1938. Note the plough carrier attached to the leading truck. (G.N.Southerden)

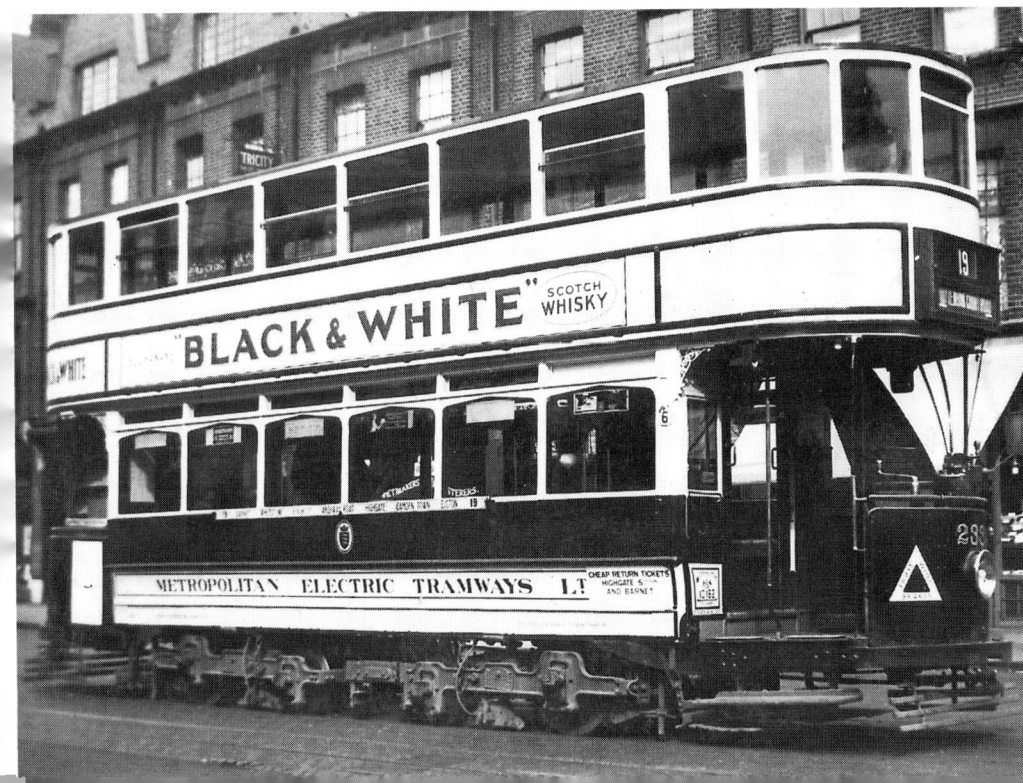

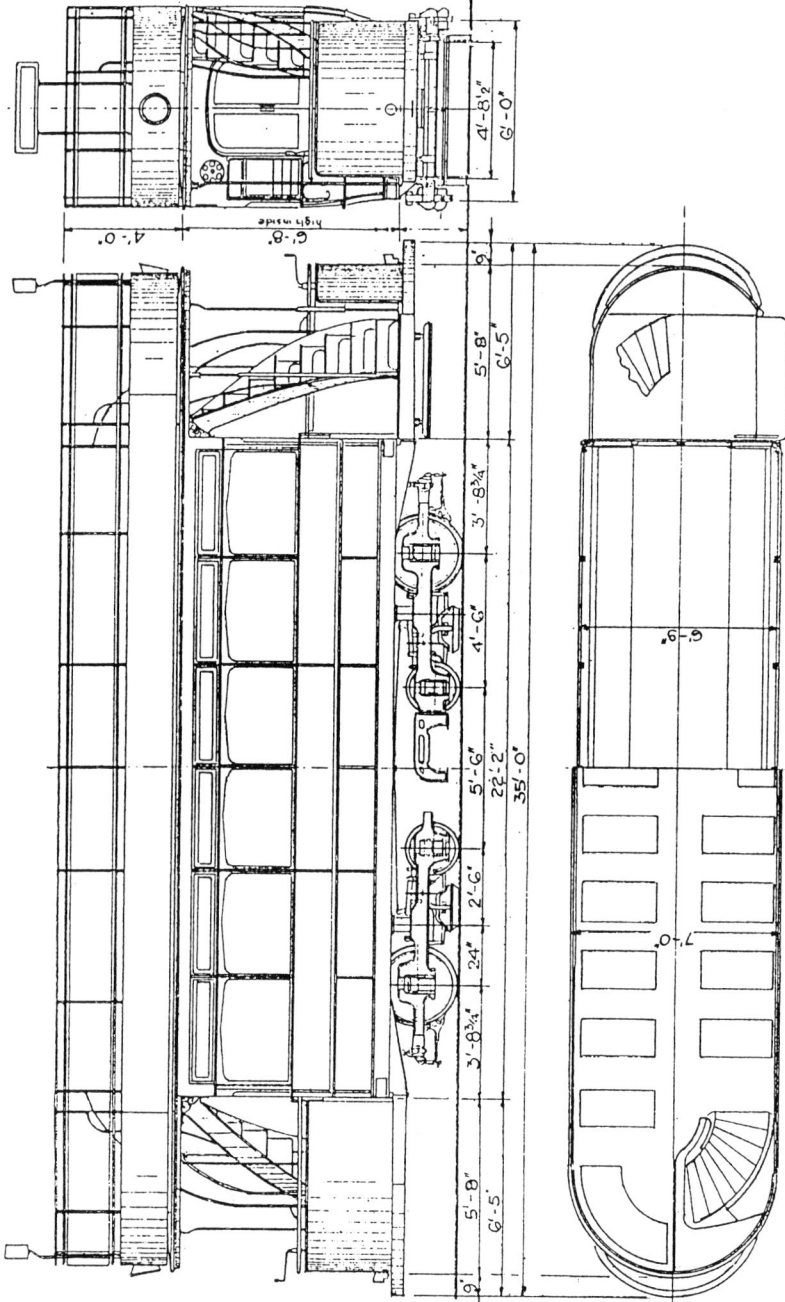

METROPOLITAN ELECTRIC TWYS.
8WHEEL OPEN TOP TRAMCAR

TYPE: 'G'

SCALE:
4 mm = 1 Foot

DRAWING No. TC 98

BODY - Brush El Eng Co Ltd

Seating 32 + 42 = 74.

TRUCKS Brush Max Ton.
Wheels 2'1¼ & 3'1½ diam.

EQUIPMENT - 2 GE Motors
Controllers, B.T.H   Trolley B.T.H

SCALE
FEET 0 1 2 3 4 5 6 7 8 9 10

4'-0"

6'-8" high inside

4'-8½"
6'-0"

9'
5'-8"
6'-5"

3'-8¾"

4'-6"

5'-6"
2'-2"

35'-0"

2'-6"
24"

3'-8¾"

5'-8"
6'-5"

9'

6'-9"

7'-0"

07. At an overall height of just over fifteen feet these cars were able to pass under the railway bridge in Turnpike Lane and were thus able to reach Muswell Hill on service 51. It is a great shame that these solid, serviceable vehicles had such a short life under London Transport. (G.N.Southerden)

Type G cars 217-236, 317.

These vehicles (cars 217-236) were built by Brush in 1909. They were originally double deck, open top trams which ran on Mountain and Gibson 3L trucks. They had seats for 32 inside and 42 outside, and all cars were first stabled at Finchley and Wood Green depots. Plough carriers were fitted in 1912-15 and in 1928-30 all type G cars were remotored and reconstructed with enclosed top covers. An extra vehicle, car 317, was added to the fleet in 1921, it was built by the MET at Hendon. Driver's windscreens followed in 1931-33 and the whole class was withdrawn in 1938. A fitting tribute to these vehicles occurs in John Barrie's *North London Tramways*, the author writes... " These cars were in my opinion the finest standard type car ever to appear on the streets of London. They compared very favourably with the rebuilt E1s (LCC vehicles) for comfort and appearance, and were certainly quieter and very much smoother riding than the latter..."

Type H

8. The date is around 1910 and car 255 is depicted in as delivered condition. Note the C route symbol and the three lamp indicator above the destination blind. (V.Whitbread)

METROPOLITAN ELECTRIC TWY.
8 WHEEL DOUBLE DECK TRAM

TYPE: 'H'

DRAWING No. TC 99

SCALE:
4 mm = 1 Foot

BODY - Brush El. Eng Co Ltd.
Seating 32 + 46 . 78

TRUCKS - Brush Max. Tr.
Wheels: 21¾ 6 31½ km

EQUIPMENT - 2 GE Motors
Controllers   BTH

SCALE
FEET 0 1 2 3 4 5 6 7 8 9 10

99. Car 284 still has the wire mesh "dog gate" between the trucks. This feature was later removed and plough carrying gear substituted when this car was taken from the Harrow Road services in 1919-20. The livery and lining details will be noted as well as the indicator boards underneath the top deck windows. (J.B.Gent Coll.)

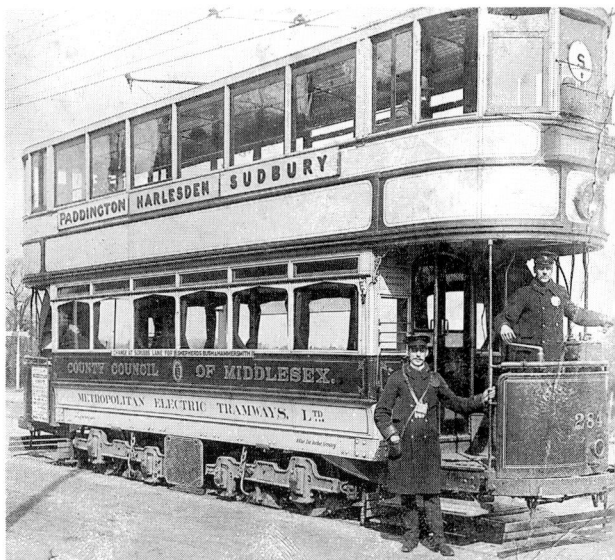

Type H cars 237-316.

Built in 1909-12 by Brush, these were double deck, enclosed top cars which ran on maximum traction trucks. They had seats for 32 passengers in the lower saloon and for 46 in the upper saloon. Most of these trams were stabled at Wood Green, Finchley and Edmonton depots. Plough carriers for cars working through services were fitted in 1912-19. From 1929 onwards there began a programme of installing driver's windscreens, although not all cars were so equipped even in the LT era. Transverse, upholstered seats were included in the modernisation scheme of 1928-30, this brought the lower saloon seating capacity down to 28 passengers. These fine cars were destined to receive the same shabby treatment from London Transport as their ex-MET sisters, the last of type H left passenger service in 1938.

100. Car 258 is seen in the late 1920s; it now possesses small side destination boards in addition to a service number indicator. (G.N.Southerden)

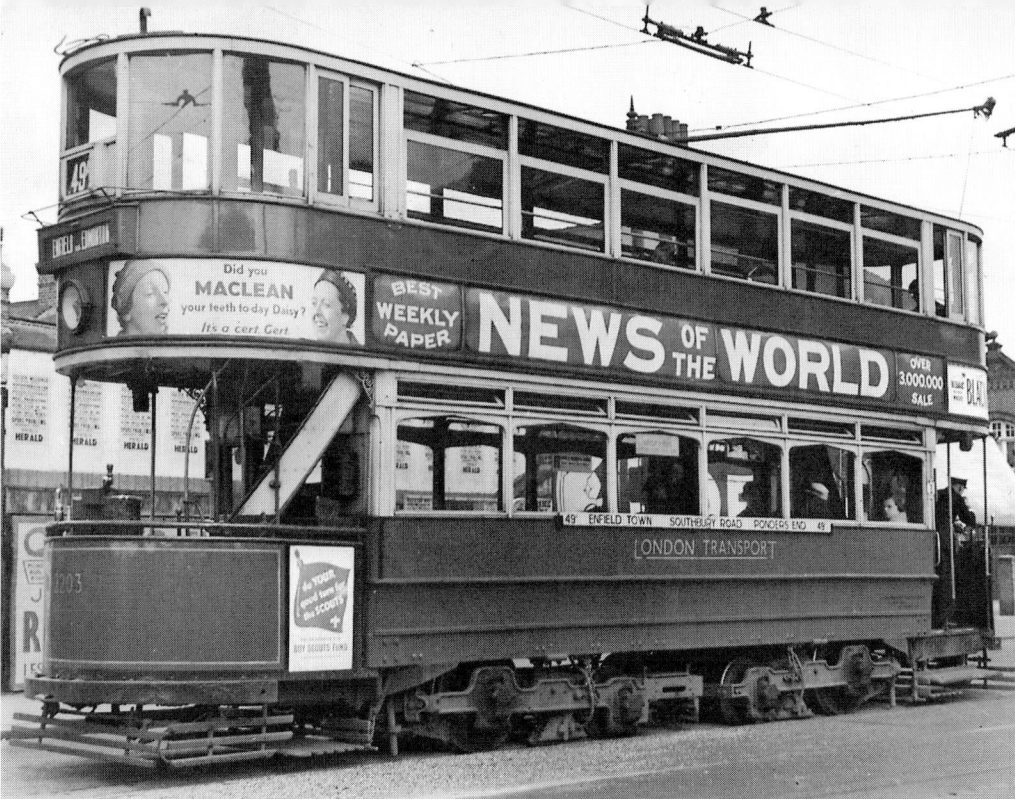

101. This vehicle is painted in the standard LT red and cream livery. It will end its days in open fronted condition. LT car 2203 was formerly MET car 271. (D.W.K.Jones)

102. Car 2203 now serves as our demonstration vehicle as we inspect the rather spartan wooden seating on the top deck. Smoking was allowed up here and quite a "fug" would build up in winter when all the windows were closed! Handrails fixed to the ceiling enabled passengers to keep their balance when they were boarding or alighting. (D.W.K.Jones)

103. The double doors leading to the lower saloon have been slid open for us to peer inside. This was the domain of the non-smokers and the upholstered seating was a definite advance on the hard wood of the upper deck. (D.W.K.Jones)

104. Car 2173 (ex-MET car 241) is depicted in its final London Transport condition; note that the headlamp is now positioned on the dash. There was a strong body of opinion amongst enthusiasts that these splendid vehicles should have been transferred south of the river to replace some of the more elderly, under-powered ex-LCC cars, but LT were having none of it and car 2173 met its nemesis in November 1938. (G.N.Southerden)

TRACK LAYOUTS -
SINGLE TRACK AND LOOPS

Some of the views in the main section of this book have portrayed single track sections. As one might expect, passenger demands on the capital's tramways required double track to be the mainstay of the system. However, at certain locations it proved impossible to effect the necessary road widening and single track had to be employed. It also has to be said that these sections sometimes caused delays especially in rush hours. Transport professionals and town planners were less likely to look with favour on this type of traffic bottleneck than the tramway enthusiast who usually relished unusual track layouts for their own sake. Whatever the merits of the argument, single line working began with G.F.Train's first London horse tramway in 1861 and was still around on the last night, 5th July 1952.

105. Some single track and loop sections could be rather tortuous - witness this scene at Milkwood Road in South London. Car 1018 twists and turns through suburban streets which are devoid of competing traffic. (J.B.Gent Coll.)

MILKWOOD ROAD

106. The first of five photos which could be titled "waiting at the loop" depicts a rather battered Bexley car 4 on the county boundary between Kent and London. The former municipal tramways of Bexley, Erith and Dartford represented some of the more dubious acquisitions which passed to LT in 1933. The single track and loop main line from Plumstead to Horns Cross was a prime candidate for replacement by a more modern form of transport. (A.H.Barkway)

107. A classic street scene of 1935 depicts a symmetrical passing loop in Plumstead. Car 1510 on service 38 waits for the tram carrying the photographer to clear the single track. The LCC made a virtue out of necessity by providing stop signs on opposite sides of the road. (G.N.Southerden)

108. On the South Metropolitan line from West Croydon to South Norwood there were around 18 passing loops to slow the service. Many views of this stretch are illustrated in *Croydon's Tramways*; here we witness two SMET cars passing. As the traffic notice indicates, there were official rules for operating in poor visability. (A.J.Watkins Coll.)

LT traffic circular for December 1935

810.—OPERATION OF CARS DURING FOG.

Notice to Staff.

The following passing places *only* are to be used during fog ; no other place may be used unless ordered by an official :—

Crystal Palace—West Croydon Route.

10 *Cars.*—Wellesley Road, " Gloster," Selhurst Station, Park Road, Portland Road, King's Road.

12 *Cars.*—Station Road, Cromwell Road, Burdett Road, Selhurst Station, Park Road, Station Road, Norwood, Goat House.

14 *Cars.*—St. Michael's Road, Spurgeon's Bridge, " Gloster," Burdett Road, Selhurst Station, Park Road, Portland Road, Norwood, King's Road.

16 *Cars.*—Station Road, Spurgeon's Bridge, " Gloster," Burdett Road, Selhurst Station, Clifton Road, Whitworth Road, Portland Road, Goat House, Selby Road.

Thornton Heath Route.

3 *Cars.*—" Brigstock Arms."

6 *Cars.*—" Brigstock Arms," Telegraph.

8 *and* 9 *Cars.*—Frant Road, Fire Station, Thornton Heath Clock.

11 *and* 12 *Cars.*—Frant Road, Fire Station, Telegraph, " Wilton Arms."

109. Like the SMET route to South Norwood, the London United Tramways line to Uxbridge was riddled with single track. Car 335 waits on Uxbridge Road, Hayes, at fare stage 19 by the Adam and Eve public house. An Amersham and District AEC Regal roars past. (G.N.Southerden)

110. Car 154 is in Lewisham Road not far from Blackheath Hill. This quiet, suburban tramway backwater used by service 58 lasted until 6th October 1951. The motorman relies on line of sight to check for oncoming trams before he proceeds. (H.B.Priestley)

111. Car 600 beats a sister car to the right of way under the railway bridge on Evelyn Street, Deptford. At many places in London the narrow road space at bridges was often the cause of single track. (R.J.Harley Coll.)

112. A two tram convoy occupies the single track in Plumstead High Street near Reidhaven Road. This 1935 view shows car 1501 on service 36 and car 1468 on service 96. This latter car was a member of class M, a four wheel vehicle only permitted by LT to run at half power over the parlous single track in the Bexleyheath and Dartford areas.
(G.N.Southerden)

113. The line in Brigstock Road, Thornton Heath retains much of its municipal charm - the spirit of Croydon Corporation survived right up to the abandonment of this section on 7th April 1951. Note the single bracket arm, the power feed and the adjacent section box. (J.H.Meredith)

114. Thicket Road, Penge is the setting for this rare view of Croydon car 9 which stands on the single track at this semi-rural terminus. (A.J.Watkins Coll.)

115. Motormen also used a line of sight driving technique on this part of Jamaica Road near Paradise Street, Bermondsey. Regulations in the 1870 Tramways Act stated that if the distance between the edge of the footpath and the nearest tram rail was less than nine feet six inches, then the frontagers could object to the construction of the tramway. (J.C.Gillham)

116. In Merton Road, Wimbledon, by Pelham Road, there existed signals to prevent two cars being on the same track. The driver of the next tram will have to wait until he sees two *diagonal* lights which indicate line clear. (C.Carter)

117. The eastbound 36 in Greenwich High Road indicates the potential dangers to other road users by its sudden swing to the left as it regains the double track. In order to minimise the risk of motorists being forced into the kerb, the TRAM PINCH sign (inset) was placed at suitable locations on London's streets. (J.C.Gillham)

118. Interlaced track was comparatively rare on the London system, but it remained here on Brigstock Road, Thornton Heath. One can only suggest it was employed at this location to save the expense of installing points. (O.J.Morris)

119. The end is nigh for cars 2188, 2250 and 2253 as they stand forlornly in Hampstead Depot. They have been ousted by trolleybuses and they now await the attentions of the blow torch and the sledgehammer. Thus the MET and these fine trams of North London passed into oblivion. (D.W.K.Jones)

120. We return to Stamford Hill for our final shot, only this time there are no trams just a trio of trolleybuses to interest us. The conductor of the leading vehicle has been somewhat wayward with his trolleypoles - perhaps he was making a personal statement to the watching LT inspector! Soon these trolleybuses will have gone and local residents will be left to wonder why so much money was wasted to produce an all diesel bus London which has contributed to fume filled roads, clogged with traffic. (C.Carter)

BRANCH LINES
Branch Line to Allhallows
Branch Lines to Alton
Branch Lines around Ascot
Branch Line to Bude
Branch Lines around Bodmin
Branch Lines around Canterbury
Branch Lines to East Grinstead
Branch Lines around Effingham Jn
Branch Lines to Exmouth
Branch Line to Fairford
Branch Line to Hawkhurst
Branch Lines to Horsham
Branch Line to Ilfracombe
Branch Lines to Longmoor
Branch Line to Lyme Regis
Branch Line to Lynton
Branch Lines around Midhurst
Branch Line to Minehead
Branch Lines to Newport
Branch Line to Padstow
Branch Lines around Portmadoc 1923-46
Branch Lines around Porthmadog 1954-94
Branch Lines to Seaton & Sidmouth
Branch Line to Selsey
Branch Lines around Sheerness
Branch Line to Southwold
Branch Line to Swanage
Branch Line to Tenterden
Branch Line to Torrington
Branch Lines to Tunbridge Wells
Branch Line to Upwell
Branch Lines around Weymouth

LONDON SUBURBAN RAILWAYS
Caterham and Tattenham Corner
Clapham Jn. to Beckenham Jn.
Crystal Palace and Catford Loop
Holborn Viaduct to Lewisham
East London Line
Lines aound Wimbledon
London Bridge to Addiscombe
Mitcham Junction Lines
South London Line
West Croydon to Epsom
Willesden Junction to Richmond
Wimbledon to Epsom

STEAMING THROUGH
Steaming through Cornwall
Steaming through East Sussex
Steaming through the Isle of Wight
Steaming through Surrey
Steaming through West Hants
Steaming through West Sussex

GREAT RAILWAY ERAS
Ashford from Steam to Eurostar
Festiniog in the Fifties

COUNTRY BOOKS
Brickmaking in Sussex
East Grinstead Then and Now

SOUTH COAST RAILWAYS
Ashford to Dover
Bournemouth to Weymouth
Brighton to Eastbourne
Brighton to Worthing
Chichester to Portsmouth
Dover to Ramsgate
Hastings to Ashford
Ryde to Ventnor
Worthing to Chichester

SOUTHERN MAIN LINES
Bromley South to Rochester
Charing Cross to Orpington
Crawley to Littlehampton
Dartford to Sittingbourne
East Croydon to Three Bridges
Epsom to Horsham
Exeter to Barnstaple
Exeter to Tavistock
Faversham to Dover
Haywards Heath to Seaford
London Bridge to East Croydon
Orpington to Tonbridge
Sittingbourne to Ramsgate
Swanley to Ashford
Tonbridge to Hastings
Victoria to Bromley South
Waterloo to Windsor
Woking to Portsmouth
Woking to Southampton
Yeovil to Exeter

COUNTRY RAILWAY ROUTES
Andover to Southampton
Bath to Evercreech Junction
Bournemouth to Evercreech Jn
Burnham to Evercreech Junction
Croydon to East Grinstead
East Kent Light Railway
Fareham to Salisbury
Frome to Bristol
Guildford to Redhill
Porthmadog to Blaenau
Reading to Basingstoke
Reading to Guildford
Redhill to Ashford
Salisbury to Westbury
Strood to Paddock Wood
Taunton to Barnstaple
Westbury to Bath
Woking to Alton

TROLLEYBUS CLASSICS
Croydon's Trolleybuses
Hastings Trolleybuses
Woolwich & Dartford Trolleybuses

TRAMWAY CLASSIC
Aldgate & Stepney Tramways
Bournemouth & Poole Tramway:
Brighton's Tramways
Bristol's Tramways
Camberwell & W. Norwood Tramw
Croydon's Tramways
Dover's Tramways
East Ham & West Ham Tramway
Eltham & Woolwich Tramways
Embankment & Waterloo Tramwa
Exeter & Taunton Tramways
Greenwich & Dartford Tramway:
Hampstead & Highgate Tramway
Hastings Tramways
Holborn & Finsbury Tramways
Ilford & Barking Tramways
Kingston & Wimbledon Tramway
Lewisham & Catford Tramways
Maidstone & Chatham Tramway
North Kent Tramways
Portsmouth's Tramways
Seaton & Eastbourne Tramways
Southampton Tramways
Southend-on-sea Tramways
Thanet's Tramways
Victoria & Lambeth Tramways
Walthamstow & Leyton Tramway
Wandsworth & Battersea Tramwa

OTHER RAILWAY BOOKS
Garraway Father & Son
Industrial Railways of the South E:
London Chatham & Dover Railw
South Eastern Railway
War on the Line

MILITARY BOOKS
Battle over Portsmouth
Battle Over Sussex 1940
Blitz Over Sussex 1941-42
Bognor at War
Bombers over Sussex 1943-45
Military Defence of West Sussex
Secret Sussex Resistance

WATERWAY ALBUM
Hampshire Waterways
Kent and East Sussex Waterway:
London to Portsmouth Waterwa
West Sussex Waterways

BUS BOOK
Eastbourne Bus Story

SOUTHERN RAILWA ● VIDEOS ●
Memories of the Hayling Island Bra
Memories of the Lyme Regis Bran
War on the Line